TILLICH: A GUIDE FOR THE PERPLEXED

TILLICH: A GUIDE FOR THE PERPLEXED

ANDREW O'NEILL

t & t clark

Published by T&T Clark
A Continuum imprint

The Tower Building   80 Maiden Lane
11 York Road   Suite 704
London SE1 7NX   New York NY 10038

www.continuumbooks.com

British Library Cataloguing-in-Publication Data
A catalogue record for this book is available from the British Library.

ISBN-10: HB: 0-567-03290-6
PB: 0-567-03291-4
ISBN-13: HB: 978-0-567-03290-4
PB: 978-0-567-03291-1

Library of Congress Cataloging-in-Publication Data
A catalog record for this book is available from the Library
of Congress.

Typeset by Newgen Imaging Systems Pvt Ltd, Chennai, India
Printed on acid-free paper in Great Britain by MPG Books Ltd,
Bodmin, Cornwall

CONTENTS

List of Abbreviations   vi

Introduction   1

PART I APOLOGETIC THEOLOGY: THE
DEVELOPMENT OF TILLICH'S APPROACH   7

1. Theological Principles: The Development
   of Tillich's Approach   9
2. Theological Method: Towards a Systematic Theology   27

PART II 'ANSWERING' THEOLOGY: QUESTIONS
OF EXISTENCE AND PROBLEMS
OF THEOLOGY   49

3. Being and God   51
4. Existence and the Christ   69
5. The Spiritual Presence and Trinitarian Thinking   83

PART III PHILOSOPHICAL THEOLOGY: CLARIFYING
THE CONCEPTUAL ROOTS OF
TILLICH'S THEOLOGY   101

6. Philosophical Concepts and Structures   103
7. Reception   124

Conclusion   131

Notes   135
Suggestions for Further Reading   152
Bibliography   153
Index   159

ABBREVIATIONS

The following abbreviations refer to the works of Paul Tillich:

BR	*Biblical Religion and the Search for Ultimate Reality* (Chicago: Chicago University Press, 1955)
CB	*The Courage to Be* (London: Nisbet, 1952)
CEWR	*Christianity and the Encounter of World Religions* (Minneapolis, MN: Fortress Press, 1994)
'*Dialectic*'	"What is Wrong with the 'Dialectic' Theology?" *Journal of Religion* XV/2 (April 1935) 127–145
DF	*Dynamics of Faith* (New York, NY: Harper Collins, 1958)
IH	*The Interpretation of History* (London: C. Scribner's Sons, 1936)
OB	*On the Boundary: An Autobiographical Sketch* (London: Collins, 1967)
PE	*The Protestant Era* (Chicago: Chicago University Press, 1957)
ST I	*Systematic Theology, vol. 1* (Chicago: Chicago University Press, 1951)
ST II	*Systematic Theology, vol. 2* (Chicago: Chicago University Press, 1957)
ST III	*Systematic Theology, vol. 3* (Chicago: Chicago University Press, 1963)
TC	*Theology of Culture,* Robert C. Kimball, ed. (New York: Oxford University Press, 1959)
'*Victory*'	'Victory in Defeat', *Interpretation* 6 (January 1952) 17–26

Other abbreviations:

EL	Hegel, G.W.F. *The Encyclopaedia Logic: Part I of the Encyclopaedia of the Philosophical Sciences,* Geraets, Suchting and Harris, trans. (Indianapolis, IN: Hackett Publishing Co. Ltd, 1991)
LPR	Hegel, G.W.F. *Lectures on the Philosophy of Religion, Volume I: Introduction and the Concept of Religion, Volume II: Determinate Religion, and Volume III: The Consummate Religion,* Peter C. Hodgson trans., ed. (Berkeley, CA: University of California Press, 1995, 1995, 1998)
SL	Hegel, G.W.F. *Science of Logic,* Vols I, II, and III (1812, 1813, 1816) A.V. Miller, trans., ed. (New York: Humanity Books, 1998)

INTRODUCTION

In the preface to *The Interpretation of History*, Tillich says that every thought must have a basis in real, historical existence,[1] and theology is no exception. Though the specifics of Tillich's theological approach changed over the course of his career, it is possible to say that, throughout, he was interested primarily in portraying the meaningfulness of revelation for humanity. He began his theological writing in the interwar period, during which the appeal of religious socialism waned and the need for a theological response to secularism and nationalism grew. He felt it necessary to re-establish the relationship between revelation and the human situation. He also sought to distinguish his theology from other efforts of the same period which, he felt, responded to social trends by simply asserting more vehemently the case for a return to Christianity. The depth of human depravity uncovered during the Second World War ensured that the theological description of human participation in the hastening of God's kingdom would have to take serious account of human fallenness, and provide an understanding of how, even amidst finitude and decay, human history can be seen as undergoing redemption.

For Tillich, the *kerygma*, or 'message' of revelation is always received in a particular context, or 'situation'. The central message of revelation may be constant, but the situation in which it is received – either as the original revelation of Jesus the Christ, or in the continued reception of this revelation through history and the Church – is constantly changing. Theology must address not only the perennial questions raised by the universal human condition, but also how and why the symbols of Christian faith meaningfully answer these questions. At the same time, theology must give an account of how human culture is expressive of these questions and answers, and how it is related to the equally human realm of religion.

To understand Tillich's theological approach it is helpful to think in terms of the two 'tasks' he sets for theology, and the two sources of the 'tools' employed to accomplish these tasks. The interwar and post-war periods are, for Tillich, dominated by the twin problems of relativism and a sense of meaninglessness. This provokes his 'apologetic' approach, which demonstrates how Christian theology responds to existential problems. In addition to the various social and political situations to which Tillich responds theologically, he also addresses what he sees as insufficiencies within theology itself. Thus, his apologetic approach includes a description of the theological criteria for self-critique and rehabilitation. These are the two major tasks of theology: responding to existence theologically while being self-critical.

The greatest challenge in Tillich's writing, however, is discerning and understanding the conceptual tools which he employs to accomplish these tasks. First, as a theologian, Tillich works within the conceptual framework of the Christian religion. The concepts and doctrines to which he most often appeals are familiar: God, Christ, the Spirit, the Trinity and the Kingdom of God. Yet, his concern to reflect on and revise contemporary theology means that Tillich cannot be placed immediately within any particular tradition of interpreting these doctrines. In fact, the notion of 'doctrine' itself is frequently replaced with 'symbol', or 'concept', in order to afford him greater latitude of description. Second, Tillich appeals not only to contemporary existential analysis to describe the modern human condition, but also to the conceptual structures of various nineteenth-century German Idealists, especially F.W.J. Schelling and G.W.F. Hegel.

It would be too strong a statement to say that he inherits, or adopts, the approach of any philosopher, but it would be too weak to say that he merely borrows certain idioms. The conceptual structures within which Tillich works owe a considerable debt to German Idealism. The interaction with philosophy is more pronounced in Tillich's early writings, especially in his two theses on Schelling, and various essays devoted to philosophical subjects.[2] However, throughout his writing Tillich continues to interact with various philosophical approaches, including those of Søren Kierkegaard and Friedrich Schleiermacher, Martin Heidegger and Jean-Paul Sartre. After his emigration to the United States, Tillich's published focus was almost solely on theology, but the concepts of being and non-being, and essence and existence, continued to dominate his theological expression.

Tillich's defining work is the three-volume *Systematic Theology*, in which the considerable conceptual tools at Tillich's disposal are brought to bear on the two considerable tasks of theology. In each section, he describes the human condition and the theological symbol that effectively addresses that situation. Human finitude, estrangement and ambiguity, the given conditions of life and history, are met and redeemed by God who, as the 'power of being-itself', appears within history as the infinite God, as the person of Jesus who is the Christ, and as the perpetual Spiritual Presence, which guides all of existence towards the goal, or *telos*, of history: salvation. Although, as we will see, there is still some debate as to whether Tillich's description of revelation successfully demonstrates the connection between human existence and the scriptural tradition, among theological statements of the human condition, Tillich's system stands out as one of the greatest of the twentieth century. His ontological approach to theology describes the underlying connection between God, who is being-itself, and human being, while his existential concern leads him to articulate the historical experience of that connection and the direction that this implies for humanity. Although we consult a majority of Tillich's publications, the outline of Tillich's theology in this book relies on the *Systematic Theology*.

Here, we will consider some of the major themes and concepts that Tillich develops to express the relationship between the human condition and the symbols through which Christian theology responds to it. In the first chapter of this book, we consider three of the principles that guide Tillich's theological thinking throughout all of his writing: theonomy, the Protestant principle and the concept of 'symbols'. Together, these principles describe the ways in which revelation simultaneously provides hope and courage, as well as the criteria for self-critical and dialectical reflection inside and outside the Church. We then describe the development of Tillich's theological method, from early discussions of boundary situations, and dialectic and paradox, through to the formal method of his mature system, the 'method of correlation' (Chapter 2). In the second section, we examine Tillich's existential interpretations of the traditional doctrines of God, Christ, the Spirit and the Trinity (Chapters 3–5). Following the structure of the *Systematic Theology*, each discussion will consider Tillich's description of the existential situation and of the Christian symbol which embodies the theological response. We will not only give each of these discussions the best reading possible, but also consider some of the main difficulties with each of Tillich's interpretations.

In order to understand and clarify the strongly philosophical nature of Tillich's theology, it is necessary and helpful to consider some of the philosophical influences operating within it (Chapter 6). Although he cites many influences on his thought, the speculative systems of Schelling and Hegel have the most bearing on the conceptual structure of Tillich's concepts of being and non-being, and essence and existence. Though the results are vastly different, the concept of dialectic and the traditional language of Christian theology figure heavily in the work of these two German Idealists. Schelling was the subject of Tillich's doctorate in philosophy and licentiate of theology, and exercises a well-documented influence on the form and content of Tillich's ontology. Although the influence of Hegel is not as clearly documented, his influence on the whole of twentieth-century theology, and on Tillich's, is apparent.

In Chapter 7, we consider some of the response to Tillich, both immediately following the publication of the three volumes of the *Systematic Theology*, and in the years following his death in 1965. Tillich has had a significant effect on many fields of study outside of theology; however, our analysis focuses on his theological significance. In this arena, the critical reaction to Tillich falls within one of two groups. In the majority are 'reparative' responses, which accept Tillich's project of interpreting theology for the contemporary situation, but are critical of his method and results. A less common 'traditionalist' response is critical of the very idea of interpreting theology in existential terms, and of its results. Since our aim is to *clarify* Tillich's central concepts, the efforts of reparative responses are more helpful and instructive.

The guiding thread throughout Tillich's theology is his insistence that the theological task, of interpreting revelation for the contemporary situation, is always self-critical. Like many of his contemporaries, Tillich argues that the experience of revelation, and subsequent theological reflection upon its authority, results in both prophetic hope and prophetic critique of the human situation. However, Tillich also argues that revelation is experienced *within* the human situation and, therefore, provides humanity the criteria for being prophetically *self*-critical. The Protestant principle represents the formal articulation of this inclination, but it is present in all of Tillich's major concepts, including theonomy, symbols, the Spiritual Community and his understanding of history. Most importantly, however, Tillich's inclination towards a self-critical principle suggests that the embracing method of correlation does not describe a finished system, but a dialectical approach to theology. His insistence upon the self-critical capacity of theology ensures that perpetual discussion, disagreement and even error are not sinful outcasts from the Kingdom, but very much a part of the dialectical history of salvation.

This relies on Tillich's assumption that the human condition is inherently capable of receiving revelation, which for some comes too close to natural theology. However, in Tillich's theological system revelation remains transcendent. It 'grasps' the human individual and community – we do not 'grasp', or finally understand, revelation. The Christ is the New Being, the revelation of authentic humanity unfettered by the confines of finitude – an authenticity we are incapable of achieving on our own. The Spiritual Presence guides human existence in its reunification with its essence – a process which requires, but cannot be accomplished by, our efforts. However, these symbols of religion also imply the universality of both the human condition and revelation. If the salvation of all humanity and history is the *telos* revealed by God, the 'power of being-itself', then all of history, culture, religion and existence are affected by and included in that promise. Ultimately, revelation is meaningful for humanity because human 'being' shares in the power of 'being-itself'.

PART I

APOLOGETIC THEOLOGY: THE DEVELOPMENT OF TILLICH'S APPROACH

THEOLOGICAL PRINCIPLES: THE DEVELOPMENT OF TILLICH'S APPROACH

Paul Tillich's approach to theology seeks to relate the content of revelation to the human experience of it. For this reason, Tillich calls his theological approach 'apologetic' or an 'answering theology'. As an 'answering' theologian, he describes this revelation to a modern audience whose experience of religion is primarily an experience of questioning its authority. Taking this concern of the wider community seriously, Tillich addresses particular theological problems and challenges, both those unique to the twentieth century, and those that persist throughout Christian history. He sets himself the task of interpreting the 'message' of revelation in such a way so as to make it relevant to the human 'situation'.

The primary way in which Tillich describes the authority of revelation is ontological. There can be no escape from the message if it is a condition of human existence itself. For Tillich, therefore, the task of theology is not to describe revelation in a way that makes it intellectually accessible to human thought; rather, the task of theology is to uncover the presence of what is revealed, or the 'unconditional', in human existence, thought and creativity.

The term 'unconditional' . . . points to that element in every religious experience which makes it religious . . . . In every symbol of the divine an unconditional claim is expressed, most powerfully in the command: 'Thou shalt love the Lord thy God with *all* thy heart and with all thy soul, and with all thy mind.'. . . Unconditional is a quality which we experience in encountering reality.[1]

In defining the revelation of what is unconditional in this way, Tillich denies that religious experience is limited to the Church. As we will see, this affects the way Tillich interprets the traditional doctrines of the Spirit and the Church.[2] The reasoning behind this definition, however, is the observation that people who participate in expressly 'religious' activities, or who have an experience of the unconditional element that makes an experience 'religious', are also people who participate in cultural activities. Indeed, history of religion, for Tillich, demonstrates the constant human activity of using stories, symbols and other cultural media to express religious ideas and concepts. Religion, therefore, receives cultural expression. Tillich even suggests that religion provides the content of culture, and culture is the form that religious content takes.[3] This not only states the interdependence of religion and culture, it also suggests that the contemporary situation Tillich addresses is one in which the boundaries between the two are less than clear.

The difficulty with a generous understanding of cultural expressions of the religious, however, is how to judge when a cultural idea, activity, or artistic expression, is genuinely expressive of the human experience of encounter with the unconditional, or revelation, and when it is not. One might ask Tillich: 'Is all culture an expression of the unconditional, or "revelatory"'? The following three sections in this chapter describe how religion and culture are related through three theologically expressed critical criteria of revelation: theonomy, the Protestant principle and the concept of symbols. In each, we see that, for Tillich, religion is not the same as revelation. Revelation is the basis of both religion and culture, such that the human experience of revelation, and the expression of this experience in religion and culture, is always tempered by an element of critique present within the experience itself.

AUTONOMY, HETERONOMY AND THEONOMY

According to Tillich, there are two basic approaches to theology which are insufficient because they reduce the content of revelation to absurdity. In earlier writing, Tillich calls them supernaturalism and naturalism; in the *Systematic Theology*, they are referred to first as supranaturalism and naturalism,[4] and later as heteronomy and autonomy; and in his final lecture on the subject, Tillich refers to them as the 'secular-rejective' and 'orthodox-exclusive' approaches

to theology. Where the language of heteronomy and autonomy provides the more formal and objective statement of Tillich's concern
regarding theological approach, we will examine the sense of some
of the related terms first.

The 'secular-rejective' approach champions the autonomy of reason and rejects the very concept of divinity, reducing the import of
Jesus the Christ to generally accepted conventional wisdom concerning ethical norms. Without the sacramental and mystical elements of
religious experience, however, theology becomes moralistic and ultimately secularized.[5] In contrast, the 'orthodox-exclusive' approach,
or 'supranaturalism', tends to preclude the potential diversity of
revelatory experience in the world by making Christ the exclusive
ground of revelation and frequently responds to the secular by imposing a derived set of norms on it.[6] The danger here is that religious
experience becomes exclusively identified with the context of revelation and not the content; idolatrous, or what Tillich calls 'demonized'.[7]
These approaches are both reductive in the same way: they reduce the
truth of revelation to a historical claim. In the secularized approach,
the facts and data of history are the only truth of the Christian
message: a good man did and said good things. In the orthodox
approach, a singular, historical event is rehearsed and preserved as
the only location of revelation. For Tillich, however, theology must
consider the unmediated universality of revelation together with the
mediated experience of revelation.[8]

Yet, religion, the human response to revelation, is historically conditioned; it struggles to express the truth of revelation within history.
Neither the religious individual nor the community can abandon
religious expression of this struggle and still claim to participate in
a process which continuously reflects on revelation. In his final lecture, *The Significance of the History of Religions for the Systematic
Theologian*, Tillich provides the simplest outline of what he calls a
'dynamic-typological', or self-critical, approach to understanding religious experience:

1. The holy is experienced within the world and recalled through
   sacrament.
2. Movements attempting to safeguard sacrament against demonization occur.
3. Prophetic criticism leads to statements of 'what ought to be'.[9]

'Sacrament' here is the human experience and identification of what is holy, the continued act of setting apart. 'Demonization' refers to the perversion of these sacraments – worshipping the experience or the finite thing as opposed to what is truly holy. Tillich suggests that resistance to demonization can be categorized into 'movements', which can have an ethical or prophetic component. The delineation of these elements should not, says Tillich, imply a progressive element in his approach to the religious experience. Rather, all three are variously present in an experience of the holy.[10]

Ultimately, religion requires a self-critical awareness of its dependence on the mediated experience of revelation.[11] Any theological approach not grounded in the experience of revelation risks becoming religion-destroying abstraction, diminishing the depth of every concrete religion. The view of religion as historical, existential and dialectical diminishes this possibility by embracing the universality of revelatory experience together with the limits of human experience. What results is a 'spiritual freedom which is both from and for one's own foundation'.[12]

The concept of secular-rejective and orthodox-exclusive approaches to theology is more formally developed in Tillich's typology of autonomy, heteronomy and theonomy, in the first volume of the *Systematic Theology*. Here, Tillich argues that reason, although it never loses its essential structure or logic, is nonetheless subject to the conditions of existence, and is, therefore, in need of revelation. The implication is that, against the assertion of the Enlightenment, reason is not blind and is, in the face of revelation, subject to criticism. To demonstrate this, Tillich describes reason in terms of competing and conflicted inclinations: autonomy and heteronomy.

Autonomy is obedience to a 'self-asserted, essential structure', or the conceptual independence of reason most associated with Enlightenment philosophy. However, Tillich suggests that, although it 'provides the structure of mind and reality', reason is nonetheless a finite human capacity 'made actual in the processes of being, existence and life'.[13] On its own it is insufficient as a grounding principle because it can only give account of itself, not the conditions under which it is manifest or their ground. The assertion of the autonomy of reason, however, is a reaction against another insufficient principle: the imposition of a heteronomous (i.e. strange) law on reason. Tillich describes heteronomy as obedience to an 'externally-asserted, reasoned structure'.

It is an authority which claims to speak in the name of the ground of being and is, therefore, able to account for reason and existence in an unconditional and ultimate way.[14] Heteronomy is historically expressed in religion and systems of law as concern primarily for the depth of reason. However, even in its claim to issue commands as to how reason should grasp and shape reality, on behalf of that depth which reason requires, the imposition of law is inherently finite. The denial of the autonomy of reason, by an externally imposed and finite law, is just as destructive as the assertion of autonomy by finite reason itself.

As a response to both the autonomy of reason and the heteronomy of religion, Tillich suggests that revelation, which Christianity takes as authoritative, is theonomous. Theonomy is not, as the name seems to imply, 'the acceptance of a divine law imposed on autonomy by a highest authority.'[15] Rather, theonomy expresses the reunion of the structural laws of reason with their inexhaustible ground, or 'depth'.[16] God is the law for both the structure and the ground of reason, thus reason and depth are properly united in God. What is united in God, however, is incomplete under the conditions of existence. Even a religion living according to divine law and making every effort to secure the freedom of reason is limited, finite, disrupted and incomplete. For Tillich, then, theonomy is not properly ascribed to any one religion or culture but to the free and original ground out of which they arise.

> Autonomy asserts that man as the bearer of universal reason is the source and measure of culture and religion – that he is his own law. Heteronomy asserts that man, being unable to act according to universal reason, must subject to a law, strange and superior to him. Theonomy asserts that the superior law is, at the same time, the innermost law of man himself, rooted in the divine ground which is man's own ground: the law of life transcends man, although it is, at the same time, his own.[17]

All thinking must struggle against the hubris that sees any human question or answer as autonomous, or any culture or religion as heteronomous. The typology of autonomy, heteronomy and theonomy suggests that self-assertion and adherence to external law are both subject to self-deception and distortion. However, a theonomous approach to existence avoids the self-deception of autonomy and heteronomy by seeking the union of the structures of reason with their depth. For Tillich, this is reason's 'quest' for revelation.

The appearance of the unity of structure and depth under the conditions of existence occurs first, not surprisingly for the Christian theologian, in the Christ.[18] However, the revelation of Christ is not an example of heteronomy because reverence for Jesus as the Christ is not reverence merely for the authority of a finite being but for divine authority. Tillich bases his argument that Jesus liberates belief from the heteronomy of a finite being on an appeal to the account in John's Gospel of Jesus saying that 'He who believes in me does not believe in *me*'.[19] Embodying self-negation, as the one who 'sacrifices the "Jesus" in him' to reveal the Christ,[20] the symbol of the Christ is the central location of the principle of theonomy.

In response to this revelation, the Church is not just a religious community which adopts, or has imposed upon it, this symbol. Rather, the Church works to become a representation of it. This is theonomy. The individual is not a religious personality but an anticipatory representation of a new reality.[21] Following the historical event of the Christ, the freedom of the Spirit continues to break through the 'mechanizing profanity' of ritual and doctrine, conquering exclusive religious claims and tragic self-elevation. Theonomy, then, represents a struggle against the frequent problems of profanization and demonization, or the reduction of religion to the merely human and the elevation of the merely human to the level of ultimate importance. Properly understood, the power of theonomous religion is not merely the confirmation of religious experience but the critiques of its interpretation, as well.

This suggests that a Church which is critical of the potential idolatry of secular life must also be critical of its own tendency towards self-elevation by means of tradition. Self-criticism is particularly evident, for Tillich, in the largely Protestant projects of the Reformation, and in the various contributions of historical criticism.[22] For this reason, Tillich associates the theonomy required of the contemporary Church with what he calls the Protestant principle.[23]

THE PROTESTANT PRINCIPLE

The theonomy that Tillich describes as the reconciliation of autonomous culture and heteronomous religion is embodied in his concept of the Protestant principle. This concept of how religion and culture must interact is a position at which Tillich arrived over a long period of time. From his earliest writings on the *kairos* of religious socialism until later statements about the uncertain future of ecclesiastical Protestantism, Tillich had been involved in numerous discussions about how the Church must respond to the political realities of his day. The idea of mutual critique of what could be broadly called Church and society arose out of a specific and tumultuous period in German history. Many churches, he felt, responded to the increasing rigidity of ideologies of the state with stronger and unhelpful statements of orthodoxy. Out of disappointment for this response, Tillich suggests that religion must embody the self-critical protest of the Reformation.

The theological discussion concerning religious socialism was at its strongest in the 1920s and early 1930s, when Tillich and others turned their attention to the crisis of faith within Germany and the rest of Europe.[24] Although the responses varied widely, theologians of this era were concerned to re-establish the validity of the Christian message in an era of increasing atheism and fascism. Religious socialism was a response based on both a fresh interpretation of the meaning of God in the midst of despair and meaninglessness, and a struggle against political ideologies during post-war reconstruction. From 1919 onwards, Tillich devoted a number of articles and lectures to this new concept of a religious socialism. One example, 'Christianity and Socialism', whose delivery brought a great deal of criticism to Tillich from Protestant quarters, demonstrates the kind of position Tillich took with respect to religion and politics in the Weimar Republic.[25] In it, he rejects any attempt to identify Christianity with a particular social order, but asserts that Christianity has a duty to shape humanity in terms of justice and liberty, and to reject oppression in any form.

Although opposed to utopianism, Tillich felt that a spirit of renewal would eventually spring out of the destruction of war. It is here that the concept of *kairos* first comes to the fore, as a moment for the eternal, or what is unconditioned,[26] to break into time and history, or what is conditioned. For Christian theology, the possibility of *kairos* is particularly located in the symbols of the Kingdom of God and of the Christ because, as we will see, each in some way surrenders its conditioned particularity in order to reveal unconditioned truth. What this looked like in terms of concrete political action is unclear. However, his association with like-minded thinkers in Berlin led to the creation of the 'Kairos Circle', a group whose discussion topics ranged from other theologians and their responses to the German situation, to the proletariat and the future of society.[27] While in Frankfurt, Tillich became associated with the *Institut für Sozialforschung*, a discussion group within the university whose members included prominent thinkers including Theodore Adorno and Max Horkheimer.[28] The general aims of the so-called 'Frankfurt School' were to revitalize Marxism apart from its practice in Russia, and to advance political criticism of the more rigid forms of socialism and nationalism gaining momentum in Europe.[29]

In the article 'Kairos and Logos: A Study in the Metaphysics of Knowledge', Tillich puts the thoughts of some of these discussions into theory and questions the validity of claims to universal truth in the face of the truth of *kairos*.[30] Given the in-breaking and unanticipated nature of revelation, the concepts by which the essence of reality is grasped are themselves changeable. This leads him to make a distinction between 'true' knowledge, which is possible, and 'absolute' knowledge, which is not. It is possible for subjective thinking to have moments of clarity, but it can never reach unconditional understanding. This, for Tillich, is the ambiguity of being witness to *kairos*: no conditioned reality can claim unconditional status.[31]

Although the context of the Protestant principle included reaction against political ideologies and entrenched authority, the spirit of it is derived from the Protestant Reformation. The Reformation, most clearly identified with Martin Luther, had pressed critique of the Church itself, not institutions outside the Church. Although the Church is the location of interpretation of the *kairos*, to Tillich's mind this did not exempt it from critique, but made it the necessary centre of self-critique. All conditioned reality, including churches and their doctrines, are subject to the critique of unconditioned reality. One of the earliest English articulations of Tillich's Protestant principle occurs in *The Interpretation of History*, in the section 'On the Boundary Between Heteronomy and Autonomy'. Here, Tillich responds to what he sees as the Barthian insistence on the heteronomy of God's Word by identifying Protestantism with constant, prophetic self-critique.

This very narrow attitude of the Barthians saved the German Protestant Church; but it created at the same time a new heteronomy, an anti-autonomous and anti-humanistic feeling, which

I must regard as an abnegation of the Protestant principle. For Protestantism is something more than a weakened form of Catholicism, only when the protest against every one of its own realizations remains alive within it. This protest is not rational criticism but a prophetic judgment. It is not autonomy, but theonomy, even if it appears, as often in prophetic struggles, in very rational and humanistic forms.[32]

The theological critique of 'pure autonomy', the Church's response to the rationalism of the Enlightenment, should not lead the Church to a new heteronomy.[33] Even a theology that firmly roots itself in scripture and in a doctrine of revelation is subject to the conflicts of human thought and the ambiguities of history. A principle of theonomy, however, represents not only a response to rationalistic autonomy, which is a concern of all twentieth-century theology, but also a protest against heteronomy in all forms, or the imposition of any absolute law other than the Great Commandment.[34] Tillich's principle abhors idolatry of any kind.[35]

This is not to suggest, however, that the religious life is somehow abandoned because of self-critique. Tillich asks, 'if protest and prophetic criticism are a part of Protestantism every moment, the question arises: How can a realization of Protestantism come about?'[36] In other words, how can religion and religious activity be organized and shared if they are meant to embody constant self-critique? For Tillich, it is religious activity itself that embodies the Protestant principle.

Realization in worship, sermon, and instruction assumes forms, which can be imparted. Ecclesiastical reality, the reality of the personal religious life, yes, even the prophetic word itself assumes a sacramental foundation, an abundance from which they live. Life cannot stand only on its own border, but it must stand also in its center, in its own abundance. The Protestant principle of criticism and protest is a necessary corrective, but is not in itself constructive.[37]

The Protestant principle cannot, on its own, sustain the religious life of participation in the experience of the holy. However, it is a grounding principle precisely because it is revealed to human thought and activity. It is the principle that guides and enables the finite freedom of a Spiritual Community seeking to fulfil the *telos* of history. Yet, it is also a humbling principle because it demands not only self-critique but also seeks to welcome critique from quarters outside the Spiritual Community.

> The Protestant principle may be proclaimed by movements that are neither ecclesiastical nor secular, but belong to both sphere, by groups and individuals who, with or without Christian and Protestant symbols, express the true human situation in the face of the ultimate and unconditional. If they do it better and with more authority than the official churches, then they and not the churches represent Protestantism for man today.[38]

This is what separated Tillich from many of his contemporaries. His concept of *kairos* permits that prophetic moments can arise at any time and in any cultural circumstance outside the Church. In this spirit, Tillich raises the question whether Protestantism, as the religion of the Protestant principle, can survive the constant critique aimed at the Church. He responds that Protestantism in the twentieth century can only survive if it continues to evaluate its symbols and objectives, deny the cleavage between sacred and profane spheres, and protest prophetically against man's attempts to give absolute validity to his own thinking and acting.[39] For Tillich, this is the relationship of religion and culture that must persist in order for the Spiritual Community to manifest the Spiritual Presence.

Writing in 1946, and reflecting on the wax and wane of religious socialism between the wars, in 'Religion and Secular Culture' Tillich describes the situation out of which the Protestant principle arose.[40] The churches of post-war Europe rejected the cultural and political revolutions as secular autonomy, while the revolutionary movements repudiated the churches as the expression of transcendent heteronomy. Religious Socialism was believed to be the answer to 'closing the gap' between religion and culture. 'History, however, has shown that it was too late for such an attempt to be successful at that time.'[41] The vision of a theonomous culture, in which the depth of ultimate concern is shown even within autonomous culture, did not come to fruition. A few years later, Tillich wrote, 'Instead of a creative *kairos*, I see a vacuum which can be made creative only if it is accepted and endured and, rejecting all kinds of premature solutions, is transformed into a deepening "sacred void" of waiting'.[42]

Yet, out of this work the idea of the religious symbol – as both not only expressive 'of that which is symbolized but also that through which it symbolized' – took root. In this concept, Tillich argues that the unconditioned towards whom a symbol points gives the symbol power, but as finite a symbol of *kairos* the symbol is also subject to change. Tillich warns that the Church, in all its denominations, must always bear this in mind. Though historical protest was essential and corrective, according to Tillich, the Protestantism of the twentieth century succumbed to the ideology of its own position. In orthodoxy and in idealism, Protestantism relives the 'sacramental and humanistic forms of the old ideologies'.[43] The answer to this is the application of its own principle, though: to fight against ideologies externally and internally. Religion and the church are no guarantee to the protestant believer.[44] So the proper response is neither for the individual to make himself the location of truth, nor the Church, but to live in the 'boundary-situation' that the Protestant principle makes possible. In this way, the symbols of faith are understood to be finite and conditioned symbols which have the power to reveal unconditioned meaning.

THE CONCEPT OF SYMBOLS

'As soon as one says anything about religion, one is questioned from two sides. Some Christian theologians will ask whether religion is here considered as a creative element of the human spirit rather than as a gift of divine revelation.'[45] So begins Tillich's *Theology of Culture*, in which he discusses religion as an ontological phenomenon and as a cosmological one. Awareness of 'the unconditioned', as present in the 'cultural and natural universe', is only possible if humanity is immediately, unconditionally and existentially grounded in 'the unconditioned'. 'Unconditioned', Tillich is careful to point out, is not synonymous with 'God', because, 'The word "God" is filled with the concrete symbols in which mankind has expressed its ultimate concern'.[46] In order for revelation to be meaningful, however, the God who reveals cannot be an object like all other objects or 'beings' but must be the 'power of being-itself'. Humanity's ontological grounding in 'the unconditioned', then, is a grounding in the power of being-itself.

Of course, there can be no genuine ontological 'awareness' without mediation. 'Awareness is also a cognitive term.'[47] Previous philosophers who attempted to articulate the mediated reception of revelation make a similar point. For example, in *The Christian Faith*, Friedrich Schleiermacher acknowledges that even the 'God consciousness', which is his term for the inherent awareness of God in human cognition, is mediated through 'particular determinations'. The unconscious sense or feeling is passively present, but once reflected upon, becomes actively mediated, or conditioned, by the act of reflection.[48] However, the priority of ontological awareness of 'the Unconditional', over a cosmological awareness, suggests a logical priority, not a temporal one. For Tillich, the important point is that humanity's awareness of that power which is unconditioned, present within the mediated world, is something that occurs within human cognition because it is always already present. This is another way that Tillich makes his stand against an overly cosmological understanding of human nature, which might argue that revelation is imposed by a God who wills it, without also arguing that humanity desires that same revelation.

The concept of 'ontological awareness' maintains that revelation can only be perceived if the God-given capacity to receive it is already inherent in the observer. This is also the basis of Tillich's understanding of faith. 'The risk of faith is based on the fact that the unconditional element can become a matter of ultimate concern only if it appears in a concrete embodiment.'[49] This embodiment includes mythological symbols and theological concepts, ritual and sacrament, demands for social justice, and even the honesty of scientific investigation. The risk of faith does not involve assertions that have greater or lesser degrees of probability for being discovered to be true in the future; it is not arbitrariness. Rather, 'faith is an existential risk', in which the concrete expressions of humanity – its cultural and religious symbols – are judged in terms of their unity or disunity with ultimate concern. The ontological approach to faith is one in which the experience of the power of being-itself is expressed by human beings in cultural *and* religious ways, and both are judged according to their proximity to that power, of which every human is inherently 'aware'.

There are consequences, for Tillich, of this existential approach. First, as we have seen, the Church is as subject to judgement as is the culture that it claims to judge. The Christ that Jesus expresses is only in unity with God if the humanity of Jesus is sacrificed in order to express the self-giving nature of God. All concrete and finite expressions of humanity are ultimately judged, and this includes the Church. Second, and as a result, the gap between sacred and secular is diminished. If all finitude is subject to the same criteria – proximity of concrete expression to the ultimate, or unconditioned power of being-itself – than what is said to be 'sacred' is not exempt in any special way from the criteria applied to that which is said to be 'secular'. Finally, the logical extension of this way of thinking, for Tillich, is that the gap between religion and culture is also diminished. Religion is an arena concerned with 'meaning', where culture is concerned with giving form or expression to meaning; in Tillich's shorthand, 'religion is the substance of culture, culture is the form of religion'.[50]

Associating culture with form and not substance may seem to make culture less meaningful than religion, but Tillich does not intend this. 'Culture' is the term Tillich gives to all those activities that give form and expression to human thought and concern. What concerns humanity 'ultimately' should be the power of being-itself, understood by humanity as God, which is traditionally the province of religion. 'Religion', however, is totally dependent on cultural forms of expression to articulate the meaning with which it is concerned. One cannot exist without the other. 'He who can read the style of a culture can discover its ultimate concern, its religious substance.'[51] The symbols of culture – especially its language, music, art and technology – demonstrate what is of greatest importance to it, its 'religion'. Similarly, the symbols of religion relate to the cultural situation what is of ultimate concern.

The doctrine of religious symbols is central to Tillich's system: how can humanity know revelation when it sees it? The use of the concept of symbols for interpretation and understanding of the content of revelation is, according to one commentator, significant enough to be Tillich's 'hermeneutic', or, the way he interprets the received tradition.[52] For Tillich, a symbol is the expressive reference point for something that is not material. That is to say, the thing to which the symbol refers is not itself available to cognition, only the symbol is. Symbols cannot be exchanged for more truthful or more accurate language. Yet, because the 'purity of reason', or the 'depth' of human cognition, is fallen,[53] humanity can only refer to truth symbolically because, in its fallen state, the human experience of truth is finite and limited.[54] The result in Tillich's system is that all religious language – including God, Christ and Spirit – is symbolic.

The only non-symbolic statement that can be made is that 'God is being-itself'.[55] This assertion is not the result of Tillich's failure or unwillingness to say anything specific about God. Rather, by Tillich's account, no theologian can say anything literal about God because to do so is to delimit God by the human incapacity for understanding. Symbols are required to express what is unconditioned because it cannot be fully grasped by conditioned forms. Consequently, the symbol cannot be further reduced or compared to that which it represents, nor can that to which it refers be grasped by some other means.[56] This implies that everything that is said about God is symbolic because it points towards God, who is the ground and structure of being. Concrete assertions use 'segments' of finite experience to refer to what is infinite. It is the nature of a symbol to be indirect, to point to the meaning it represents and, in the face of that meaning, to be negated. For this reason, a symbol is always finite and changeable. It has truth, insofar as it correlates a person with final revelation; and it is true, insofar as it is the expression of a true revelation. The only thing that remains constant is that God is the source and structure of all being and is, therefore, non-symbolic.

'God is being-itself' is the logical, non-symbolic reality that grounds the possibility that other things are, and that in their existence they refer to God. Yet even this statement cannot, by its logical necessity as guarantor, confine God to an ontological necessity. In fact, elsewhere Tillich says that everything we say about God symbolic.[57] This would seem to imply that the statement 'God is being-itself' is itself symbolic. Some clarification is required. To begin with, the term 'God' is symbolic. Thus the statement 'God is being-itself' cannot be completely non-symbolic. One commentator has suggested that the statement 'God is being-itself' actually relates two 'first-order' statements in a 'second-order' theological reflection.[58] 'God' is a first-order religious statement; it is symbolic. 'Being-itself' is a first-order ontological statement and is non-symbolic, or literal. The correlation of the two, in the statement 'God is being-itself,' is a second-order statement which is literal, but which correlates a symbolic statement with a non-symbolic statement. In short, 'Religious assertions are symbolic . . . ontological assertions are literal . . . and theological assertions are literal descriptions of the correlation between the religious symbols and the ontological concepts'.[59] not a Tillich quote

We can also view the statement 'God is being-itself' in terms of Tillich's efforts to position revelation as ontologically relevant. The connection between God and humanity, between essential human nature and existence, is conceptually achieved through the polarity of being and non-being. In essence, these are balanced; in existence, they are not. Because of this inherent connection, humanity is capable of having an experience of the revelation of undisrupted essence, even though it is incapable of understanding it, defining it or conceiving of its nature. These two assertions are not contradictory.[60] It is possible to have a vague sense of something without being able to form a clear concept of it. Similarly, we do not have a clear conceptual grasp of God as being-itself and cannot, therefore, make literal statements about it. We do, however, have an ontological awareness of God as being-itself and an experience of revelation 'grasping' the human mind, which we express in theological statements, or symbols.

The language of symbol, then, is not a less fulsome or less faithful alternative to 'a metaphysical account of the inner life of a divine being'.[61] All words and concepts that refer to God, and thereby the persons of the Trinity, are ultimately symbolic because none of them can exhaustively describe their referents. Theology is bound by the finite human capacity to describe and Tillich wants to ensure that what theology refers to is not also bound by that finitude.[62] A symbol participates in a deeper meaning, which it represents, by conveying that which is otherwise inexpressible.[63] Theologians must employ symbols because, 'on the one hand theology has a *meditative* task, to experience the power of the symbols; on the other a *discursive* function to analyse and describe the form in which the substance can be grasped'.[64]

Although symbols, for Tillich, are always constrained and finite, they are never 'merely' symbols, because that to which they refer is unconstrained and infinite.[65] 'A symbol participates in the reality it symbolizes', but most importantly this allows the Christian to, for example, '[participate] in the New Being as it is manifest in Jesus the Christ'.[66] The vagueness of what Tillich means by 'participation' is still a topic of debate.[67] However, it is clear that, 'The function of the religious symbol is to mediate between being-itself and man's concern with the concrete, to make present being-itself in a thinkable, finite object, to which one can relate and about which one can be concerned'.[68] However, for Tillich, symbols should never be substituted by a more scientific, or literal, expression,[69] nor should they be taken literally. The symbol is the 'adequate and necessary vehicle for communicating and experience of revelation'.[70]

What makes a symbol adequate and necessary? It is clear from what he says about the self-negation of the Christ, and the prophetically critical role of the Spiritual Presence in the community, that a symbol of revelation is not merely a conveyor of data, but a finite expression which is capable of revealing the infinite through its own self-negation. For this reason, the central symbol of the Christian faith is the absolute paradox of the Cross.[71] Jesus only becomes the Christ through his sacrifice; the unconditioned becomes a conditioned reality, unites itself with the human condition, and reveals the unconditioned in a way not possible without this paradox. The symbol of the Christ, as self-negation, is the basis of the Protestant principle, the courage to be in the face of anxiety and meaninglessness, and the expression of New Being as the redemption of estrangement.

The symbol of the Christ is also associated with the concept of *kairos*. As we have seen, the *kairos* is the central event of history in which the power of being-itself is revealed, and which gives meaning to various other *kairoi* in history. The symbol of the Christ as absolute paradox, as the revelation of the unconditioned within the conditions of existence, therefore, is what gives meaning to other possible moments of revelation. Interestingly, it is this concept of absolute paradox that allows Tillich, in his last lecture, to make a powerful statement concerning the inclusivist nature of the Christian symbol of the Christ. He says that what happened in the event of the Cross in a symbolic way also happens elsewhere, though fragmentarily, in other moments, even those not connected with the Cross.[72] The Christ is the symbol of 'final revelation', that is, the ultimate criterion of all revelation, and all other events and symbols can only participate in his truth 'fragmentarily' because only this one symbol has 'the power of negating itself without losing itself'.[73] Nonetheless, it is as *the* symbol of divine self-manifestation and as the self-negation of what is conditioned that the Christ brings unconditional meaning to other moments of revelation.

There is some suggestion that Tillich's notion of symbol does not accomplish more than any other concept of religious language might. Symbols supposedly 'mediate the power of Being-Itself and so are revelatory, and Tillich says that revelation is salvation'.[74] Yet for Tillich, it is 'events, persons and things', not words, that are the carriers of revelation. The problem is in what way symbols, which are human words and concepts used to refer to revelatory experience, can be any more meaningful or any more the bearer of meaning than words can be.[75] Perhaps, the concept of symbols could be very simply replaced with a notion of religious language as metaphorical. For Tillich, however, symbols and metaphor do not perform the same task.

It could be that for Tillich 'metaphor' captures a helpful sense of description, but not participation. It could also be that Tillich's emphasis on 'symbol' has more to do with his distinction between symbols and signs, where the sign merely points to meaning, while the symbol is an embodiment of meaning. For example, 'the American flag' is a sign, but the 'United States of America' is a symbol. One cannot participate in the flag; one can participate in the United States of America.[76] Metaphor can be used to describe both signs and symbols, but it cannot do the work of providing the distinction that Tillich intends between description and participation.

A more likely interpretation of Tillich's insistence on the concept of symbols, rather than metaphor, comes from the difference in the essential power of human words and of the Divine Word. In the third volume of the *Systematic Theology*, Tillich describes life in terms of three processes. In self-integration, the centre of the subject's awareness, critique and alteration is itself.[77] In self-creation, new centres are created and the individual is understood as a social being.[78] In self-transcendence, the individual and the community are understood in relation to the inexhaustible source of meaning: God.[79]

Tillich further describes language as the medium of self-creation, which is the second function of life under the dimension of the Spirit.[80] The symbol, however, is the medium of self-transcendence, mediating between the divine and the human. This suggests that the symbol, as participation in the revelation of being-itself, is the bearer of something more than language can be. Languages always both reveal and conceal,[81] but for Tillich, 'Where there is spirit, there estrangement in terms of language is overcome – as in the story of Pentecost'.[82] Distortion and estrangement are overcome when the human word gives way to the Divine Word.[83] The Spirit's presence is mediated by ordinary words,[84] but the Spirit is not bound by particular words. This implies that all literature, not only the Bible, can communicate the Word of God.[85]

The difference between symbol and language is reminiscent of Tillich's understanding of the Church. Like the Church, human language does not itself possess the power of self-critique and transformation; it depends on the symbols of revelation to include a transcendent critique. The implication is not that human language cannot be self-critical and adaptable. Rather, the capacity for critique and adaptation ultimately lies not within language itself, or within reason, but with the power of Being. The concerns here for Tillich, as in the whole of the *Systematic Theology*, are divine freedom and the sin of human self-elevation. Symbolic statements about God, like 'Christ' and 'Spirit', are symbolic not only because they point to or reveal the infinite, but also because they have the ability to change and still reveal the infinite.

CHAPTER TWO

THEOLOGICAL METHOD: TOWARDS
A SYSTEMATIC THEOLOGY

For Tillich, the duty of every theology is 'to address itself to the contemporary mind'. If this goal is maintained from the outset, theology
can avoid two contradicting, but related, errors: supernaturalism and
naturalism. 'The first makes revelation a rock falling into history
from above, to be accepted obediently without preparation or ade-
quacy to human nature. The second replaces revelation by a structure
of rational thought derived from and judged by human nature.'[1]
Tillich's response to these two approaches is what he calls the 'method
of correlation', in which the 'question' of existence is formulated
largely with the help of philosophical analysis and the social sciences,
and the 'answer' is communicated through the interpretation of revelation as described in the symbols of the Christian faith.[2] 'The answer,
of course, must be interpreted in light of the question, as the question must be formulated in light of the answer.'[3] Tillich's hope in
correlating existential and theological analysis is to overcome the
limitations of a discussion caught between 'fundamentalism or neo-
orthodoxy' on one hand and 'theological humanism or liberalism' on
the other. In order to understand the 'method of correlation' for
which Tillich became known, however, it is necessary to consider
some earlier articulations of his commitment to relating existential
and theological insights.

So encompassing is Tillich's view on the religious nature of all thought
and experience that it is not clear what, if anything, falls outside the
scope of interest for the systematic theologian. He is quoted to have
said at the beginning of a lecture, 'There is no such thing as Religious
Existentialism because there is only Religious Existentialism.'[4] One
commentator has suggested that Tillich's correlative approach is the

result of three distinct concerns. First, Tillich always wrote with the contemporary cultural situation in mind. This means that the task of interpreting the message of revelation for the human situation 'meant for Tillich something different in 1919 than in 1926 or 1934 or 1956.'[5] Yet, it also means that correlation is always an experientially grounded activity. Second, his interest in a correlational theology arises out of an interest to prevent the bifurcation of religion and culture in general, though not necessarily to equate the two.[6] Finally, his enterprise has predecessors in a tradition of nineteenth-century philosophical theology, who 'accepted the challenge given by Schleiermacher to develop a theology of mediation between religion and culture'.[7]

Tillich's approach is varied and adaptable. This not only makes hard work for tidy definitions of what the method of correlation is, but also makes it necessary to look at correlation as a faceted concept, rather than a monolithic one. In what follows, we will see the idea of correlation expressed in three ways: as the interaction between related fields of thought related within 'boundary situations'; as the 'dialectic' of revelation, *kerygma*, or 'message', and human experience, or 'situation'; and as the formal 'method of correlation', which seeks to answer existential questions with theological content.

BOUNDARY SITUATION

One of Tillich's earliest descriptions of the theological task occurs in the first part of *The Interpretation of History*, in which he autobiographically outlines some of the experiences and situations of his own life that informed his theological approach. The section titled 'On the Boundary' contains descriptions of his home life, his education, and his experiences in political activism in Germany before and after the First World War. It also contains descriptions of 'boundary situations', or arenas of interaction between related concepts. Three situations are of central importance to Tillich's theological approach: the boundaries between philosophy and theology, Church and society, and religion and culture. In each pair, Tillich describes a relationship in which traditional categories and boundaries are redefined by the contemporary theological and cultural situation. As a result, it is not the content of revelation that changes, but the understanding of it, in accordance with the situation in which it is received.

In the first boundary situation, between theology and philosophy, Tillich describes his lifelong passion for philosophy, particularly the post-Idealist existential responses to Neo-Kantianism evident in Kierkegaard and Heidegger, and its pervasive influence on his theology. He emphasizes the appeal of Schelling's 'philosophy of existence' over Hegel's 'philosophy of essences'; a characterization typical of the early twentieth-century disenchantment with Hegel. For Tillich, the 'philosophy of religion is not only determined by the religious reality but also by the philosophical concept'. That is not to say that the content of revelation is structured by philosophical concepts. Rather, the discipline of theology is shaped by the methods of philosophical self-critique. At this early stage in his American career, Tillich is asserting that, although its content and sources of authority differ from philosophy, theology is a rational discipline that depends on philosophical concepts.

In the second boundary situation, Tillich conceptualizes the Church according to a change in its traditional function within society. He distinguishes between the 'manifest' church, or the public institutions defined as churches, and the 'latent' church, or the inclination present within many groups in the wider society that have opted out of institutional allegiance in favour of a Christian humanism. For Tillich,

> It will not do to designate as 'unchurched' all those who have become alienated from organized denominations and traditional creeds. In living among these groups for half a generation I learned how much of the latent Church there is within them. I encountered the experience of the finite character of human existence, the quest for the eternal and the unconditioned, an absolute devotion to justice and love, a hope that lies beyond any Utopia, an appreciation of Christian values and a very sensitive recognition of the ideological misuse of Christianity in the interpretation of Church and State. It has often seemed to me that the 'latent Church', as I call what I found among these groups, was a truer church than the organized denominations, if only because its members did not presume to possess the truth.[8]

The traditional distinction between what qualifies as being 'sacred' or 'profane' is no longer sufficient, for Tillich. In his experience, non-Christian groups are politically and socially active in ways consistent with the values and principles espoused by the Church.

The final boundary situation is the relationship between religion and culture. As in the case of theology's use of philosophical concepts, Tillich suggests that the 'content' of religion cannot be expressed without cultural 'forms'. However, in this case, Tillich asserts that the content of religion is also present in cultural expressions, particularly art and music. Tillich encourages the reader to try to categorize an experience of the mosaics of Ravenna or of the Sistine Chapel as either religious or cultural. Of course, he says, they are both, as the viewer is moved by both the form of the work and by the content it portrays. He suggests that all cultural forms share this characteristic:

> It might be correct to say that the experience is cultural in form, and religious in substance. It is cultural because it is not attached to a specific ritual act; but it is religious because it touches on the question of the Absolute and the limits of human existence. This is as true of music, poetry, philosophy and science as it is of painting.[9]

The art form, cultural expression, or 'symbol', cannot be expressive only of itself, for Tillich, because it depends not only on its content for substance, but also on the observer for meaning. As a result, the observer of the cultural form participates in something greater than the form itself, and the experience can be religious. 'Wherever human existence in thought or action becomes a subject of doubts and questions, wherever unconditioned meaning becomes visible in works which only have conditioned meaning in themselves, there culture is religious.'

In these three situations, the experience of the boundary situation is different. However, there is a consistent theme: participation in cognition and existence involves a tension between categorization, and the sublimation of categories. A concept is only helpful insofar as it allows the thinking subject both to understand and to critique. Thus, there is a dialectical relationship between theological and philosophical concepts, between traditional and contemporary visions of the Church, and between religious themes and their myriad cultural expressions. Tillich acknowledges, and even encourages, that this prevents the neat categorization of existence. 'To stand on many border lines means to experience in many forms the unrest, insecurity, and inner limitation of existence, and to know the inability of attaining serenity, security, and perfection.' Throughout Tillich's subsequent writings, the unrest of existence and the elusiveness of perfection provide the challenge and quest of human existence.

The problem with the boundary situation approach to theology is its vagueness. There is a tension inherent in the dialectical relationship of concepts shared by different disciplines, which Tillich acknowledges.

> This is the dialectic of existence; each of life's possibilities drives of its own accord to a boundary and beyond the boundary where it meets that which limits it. The man who stands on many boundaries experiences the unrest, insecurity, and inner limitation of existence in many forms . . . [but] there remains a boundary for human activity which is no longer a boundary between two possibilities but rather a limit set on everything finite by that which transcends all human possibilities, the Eternal.[10]

The roots of this inclination towards crossing cognitive boundaries run deep in Tillich's formative education, especially in his early study of Schelling and Hegel. The prevalence of German Idealism in Tillich's thought is palpable in the above quotation. Existence is a dialectical experience, not only within the limits of cognition and experience, but also between the conscious limits of existence and the 'Eternal', which is unlimited. In early American publications of his writings, Tillich names the Kingdom of God as the 'eternal' that simultaneously sets and transcends limitation;[11] later, it is the very power of being-itself that sets and transcends limits.[12] We examine later how Tillich's appeals to dialectical patterns of thinking differ substantially from those of German Idealism. Nevertheless, Tillich's use of dialectic is a critical aspect of his entire theological approach.

DIALECTIC AND PARADOX

In the *Systematic Theology*, Tillich repeatedly refers to the necessity of taking a 'dialectical approach' to theology. He offers not so much a reason why, but seems to assume that concepts of truth, authority, revelation, ontology and existence require such an approach. Tillich often describes dialectic as a 'discussion' in which both 'Yes and No' can be applied to theological statements, ensuring that theology does not 'join the chorus of those who live in unbroken assertions'.[13] In this sense, dialectic is an informal inclination rather than a formal method. However, we will see that the concept of dialectic also provides the more formal structure of the *Systematic Theology* in two distinct ways. First, dialectic describes the polarity of 'being and non-being' which is the source of conflict and opposition inherent in cognition and existence. This allows Tillich to describe revelation as the power of undisrupted 'being-itself' that 'grasps' existent being and reason, rescuing it from the intractable polarity of existence and the inherent conflicts and ambiguities of human life and history.

Second, a threefold dialectic provides the overarching structure of Tillich's system, which culminates in a description of the historical process of 'essentialization'. Tillich describes the universal human condition, of finitude and hope for redemption, conceptually. The *imago dei*, or authentic human nature, Tillich refers to as its 'essence'. Humanity living under the condition of 'sin', which Tillich describes as finitude, estrangement and ambiguity, is human 'existence'. Tillich calls the possibility of existence being reunited with essence the process of 'essentialization'. The triad of essence, existence and essentialization corresponds to traditional theological doctrines of pre-Fall Creation, fallen humanity and the Kingdom of God. Each stage of this triad is also related to a person of the Trinity, or a manifestation of the 'power of being-itself': God creates perfect human essence; the Christ redeems fallen human existence; and the Spiritual Presence guides the essentialization, or reconciliation, of historical, human existence with its essence.

In the *Systematic Theology*, then, dialectic describes both the polarized conflict of imbalanced being and non-being in existence, and the triadic process of reconciling finitude, estrangement and ambiguity, or 'salvation'. In both cases, the 'message' of revelation 'grasps' the individual and spiritual community in such a way that the 'situation' of existence and history are gradually redeemed from conflict and ambiguity. Before considering the place of dialectic within the *Systematic Theology*, however, we must consider the origins of this particular concept in relation to Tillich's correlational approach to theology.

Dialectic is foundational for Tillich's apologetic approach to the message of revelation and its relevance for human cognition and history. The centrality of dialectic to the task of theological repair is stated clearly in an article written around the time of Tillich's emigration to the United States. Here, he challenges Karl Barth's definition of 'dialectical theology', on the basis that it does not

include humanity's participation in the reception of revelation.[14]
Tillich argues that Barth's description of God's simultaneous 'yes'
of salvation and 'no' to sin do not form a dialectical relationship.
Because both yes and no come from God, Tillich contends that revelation, for Barth, is a one-sided pronouncement uttered against an
entirely fallen humanity. Barth's insistence on the complete inability
for humanity to cognitively approach God, says Tillich, makes a
human question about God impossible. In the *Systematic Theology*,
Tillich likens such an understanding of revelation to a stone 'thrown
at' the human experience.[15] The question of whether Barth's use
of 'dialectic' is the same throughout his career is the subject of continued discussion,[16] as is Tillich's interpretation of Barth's use of
dialectic. However, Tillich's understanding of dialectical theology in
contrast with others' is significant.

For Tillich, as for Barth, revelation is beyond human understanding. Theology, however, is a human endeavour. The 'dialectics' of a
dialectical theology, therefore, refers to the method by which human
thought seeks a clearer understanding of its experience of revelation.
By means of positing, reflection and critique, a dialectical theology
should enable its participants to move closer to an understanding of
what revelation means for humanity. For Tillich, Barth has taken the
concept of 'yes' and 'no', which should refer to theological discussion, argument and dispute, and has placed them in the inaccessible
realm of divine judgement.

Tillich's understanding of the function of dialectic in human
reflection on revelation is consistent throughout his writing, from his
article on Barth through to the *Systematic Theology*. First, in the
introduction to *The Protestant Era*, Tillich says that

> dialectics is the way of seeking for truth by talking with others
> from different points of view, through 'Yes' and 'No,' until a 'Yes'
> has been reached which is hardened in the fire of many 'No's and
> which unites the elements of truth promoted in the discussion.[17]

Second, in *Biblical Religion and the Search for Ultimate Reality*,
Tillich says,

> Through 'Yes' and 'No,' errors are overcome and reality discloses
> itself to the mind . . . [one] transcends even them and tries to reach
> being-itself, the ultimate aim of thought. He does this, not in order

to define it – which is impossible, since it is the presupposition of every definition – but to point to that which is always present and always escaping.[18]

Finally, in the *Systematic Theology*, Tillich further clarifies his understanding of dialectic against a concept he feels is often confused with dialectic: paradox. 'One element drives another', in dialectic, even if they appear to contrast each other initially.[19] Dialectical opposition is more like a discussion that is never finished, and it is this dynamism that maintains the rationality of dialectic on the one hand. Paradox, on the other hand, while not of necessity irrational, says Tillich, nonetheless represents assertions, either of single or paired concepts, that do not permit discussion.[20] A paradox must be singularly accepted or rejected, while dialectic is continuously pursued.

This contrast of dialectic and paradox helps us to understand the early distinction Tillich makes between his understanding of dialectic and what he perceives as Barth's. For Tillich, a dialectical approach to theology includes human participation in a discussion in which revealed truth can be understood and misunderstood, interpretations proposed and countered. Human participation in the event of revelation does not imply that the truth of revelation can be derived, or that knowledge of God can ever be conclusive.[21] Tillich is clear in his article about Barth and in the *Systematic Theology* that humanity's question about God presupposes God's presence as the answer: revelation. This means that revelation is not immanently attainable through reason. The human experience of revelation can only occur because what is transcendent 'has already dragged us out beyond ourselves'.

The problem for Tillich is that 'Barth leaves unexplained how revelation can communicate anything to man if there is nothing in him permitting him to raise questions about it, impelling him towards it, and enabling him to understand it.'[22] If Tillich has correctly understood Barth's concept of dialectic, then Barth's assertion of the divine utterance of a simultaneous 'yes' and 'no' is an exclusively divine activity. If revelation is only a divine pronouncement at humanity that cannot be understood, then Barth's concept of revelation is not actually dialectical, but paradoxical – it represents a pair of truths which must be accepted simultaneously.

The question of difference between dialectic and paradox, then, is focused on the epistemological question of the reception of revelation:

by what criteria does humanity know to take revelation as authoritative? For Tillich the criteria reside within the shared essential nature
of divinity and humanity. Tillich objects to what he perceives as
Barth's devaluation of both human knowledge and the human pursuit of understanding. He agrees that human knowledge is fallen and
often quite faulty, especially when it comes to knowledge of God.
However, he does not agree that finite knowledge of God implies
complete ignorance; even errant knowledge has a dialectical value,
otherwise the whole history of religion is thus transformed into a
'Witches' Sabbath of ghostly fantasies, idolatry and superstition'.[23]
Tillich's fundamental objection to what he sees as a Barthian definition of dialectic is its characterization of the impossibility of human
knowledge of God, when 'dialectic' should imply participation and
the possibility of knowledge, even if finitely and errantly. Tillich,
therefore, prefers to refer to Barth's 'yes' and 'no' of revelation as
paradoxical, but not dialectical.

This should not be taken as Tillich's rejection of Barth's theology
of grace, however. In the *Systematic Theology*, Tillich also makes use
of a concept of paradox, as that which 'contradicts the *doxa*, the
opinion which is based on the whole of ordinary human experience,
including the empirical and the rational'.[24] Specifically,

> The Christian paradox contradicts the opinion derived from man's
> existential predicament and all expectations imaginable on the
> basis of this predicament. . . . The appearance of the New Being
> under the conditions of existence, yet judging and conquering
> them, is the paradox of the Christian message.[25]

Tillich agrees that God's choice to reveal Godself to fallen humanity
is an act of grace. God's salvation of sinful humanity is not conse-
quential or necessary, but is the result of God's paradoxical grace
towards humanity.[26] Tillich suggests that the strength of Barth's
theology is the grace inherent in his concept of God's 'dialectical yes
and no'. Salvation through revelation is, as Barth says, an 'impossible
possibility', one that humanity cannot predict or account for of its
own merit. On this, Tillich agrees with Barth. Thus, it is clearly the
concept of dialectic that Tillich is aiming to clarify.

The appearance of the Christ who conquers existence under the
conditions of existence is a paradox – it cannot be made sense of
by human rationality. Paradox has a central and logical place in

Christian theology because it simultaneously asserts the particular manifestation, or 'fact', of God in the human person of Jesus, and the unknowability of God, or transcendent origin of the 'act' of revelation.[27] The paradox of grace expressed in the Christ subverts the standard 'opinion' (*doxa*) that a thing or event can be either particular or transcendent but not both at the same time.[28] The human experience of revelation as paradox ensures divine transcendence while maintaining the certainty that revelation is for humanity.[29]

Yet, a truly dialectical theology, as Tillich conceives of it, also ensures that errant human knowledge is not entirely devalued and remains related to the existential experience of God's revelation. The paradox of God's revelation in Christ is, therefore, a paradoxical moment within a much longer dialectical process; a process that includes both the human reception of revelation and the attempts to understand and live out a response to that revelation.[30]

Tillich's understanding of paradox has met with some objection, though in some cases this is due to assumptions regarding Tillich's definition and use of the term. The main criticism is that Tillich claims to 'observe' paradox and, thereby, understand and transcend it. In trying to maintain both the paradoxes of faith and the solutions of dialectical reason, some suggest that Tillich ends up explaining paradox away.[31] Others insist that paradox is the faith of the individual who does not know and therefore believes.[32] The rational demonstration of the need for paradox diminishes its power of breaking into ordinary experience from above.

Such concern may be overstated, as Tillich explicitly says that all other doctrine rests on paradox.[33] First, it is employed in order to secure the transcendence of revelation, not to qualify what must remain absolute. Second, the paradox *of faith* for the individual, to believe 'though he has not seen', is not exactly what Tillich is referring to. For him, paradox refers to the incomprehensibility of the divine manifestation, not the contrast of faith and cognition in the believer. If anything, Tillich's notion of the paradox of grace, which coincides with Barth's, reinforces the simultaneous reality of human sinfulness and divine salvation. He is clear that the human situation demands something that is beyond its experience, but that, because of its finitude, reason cannot imagine for itself what form this might take.[34] As we will see, even the capacity for reason which is associated with faith is something for which neither human reason nor logic are responsible.

Before the *Systematic Theology*, Tillich's insistence on 'dialectical' theology refers to the need for human participation in discussion about the experience of revelation. The frailty of human wisdom should not preclude human participation in the effort to receive, understand and interpret revelation. However, when Tillich's theological approach culminates in the *Systematic Theology*, his dialectical approach to theology becomes more formal and structured. In the first volume, a dialectical relationship between being and non-being is the source of essential stability and existential imbalance. In the second volume, dialectic describes the manifestation of existential imbalance in the competing inclinations of the human individual. In the third volume, however, dialectic describes the triadic shape of the history of salvation.

THE METHOD OF CORRELATION

In the first volume of the *Systematic Theology*, the boundary situations on which Tillich reflects personally in *The Interpretation of History*, and the dialectical approach to which he refers in earlier works, are described more fully. The categories of theology and philosophy, in particular, are incorporated within a larger framework of question and answer, and the relative responsibilities of the two disciplines, in the human and theological task of 'answering' the questions of existence, is delineated. On the surface, the structure of the *Systematic Theology* appears, simply, to place a philosophical concept next to a theological one: 'God' with 'Being', 'Christ' with 'Existence' and 'the Spirit' with 'Life'. However, the method of correlation has more specific tasks in view.

According to Tillich, theologians work within an arena of commitment, a 'theological circle'.[35] They are bound within a covenant of faith to study, interpret and spread the Christian *kerygma*, the unchangeable truth or 'message' of Christ. This message is communicated through the source of Scripture, mediated by experience and attested to under the norm of baptismal confession. Though it is not irrational, theology's transmission of this message is constrained by particular historical and cultural contexts, what Tillich calls the human 'situation'. Thus, theology must responsibly transmit the eternal truth of the Christian Gospel and attend to the changing demands of the situation in and to which it is transmitted. This means that an 'answering' theology addresses two questions: the human 'quest' for a revelatory unburdening of existence and the problems present in theological responses already articulated.

Thus, Tillich makes use of philosophical concepts, throughout his writing but especially in the *Systematic Theology*, to articulate revelation's 'answer' to the human 'question' of existence. The use of these concepts, though, is not an effort to replace the content of theology with reason or to 'rationalize' theology. Rather, Tillich employs philosophical 'tools' he finds helpful in addressing the central problems of contemporary theological responses to the human situation. Philosophy helps in posing the question of existence, but it is, ultimately, theology whose content is revelation, which can alone provide the answers. Correlation is a theological assertion.[36] Not only in the *Systematic Theology*, but also evident in most of his writings, Tillich posits the three main problems facing theology, both from within and from outside, as supranaturalism, naturalism and dualism.

The term Tillich uses as both the noun that is theology's object, and the adjective which describes its motivation, is 'ultimate concern'. This is not to be confused with terms that sound similar, such as 'unconditioned', 'infinite' or 'highest thing'.[37] While Tillich does describe 'ultimate concern' as an abstraction of the Great Commandment, 'it is not arguable in detached objectivity'.[38] As the object of theology, *ultimate* concern is inevitably transcendent of all other finite concerns. Yet as ultimate *concern*, says Tillich, it is an existential concept that implies the relationship of humanity to that which determines its very being and the possibility of not-being, life and death.[39] Tillich also refers to 'ultimate concern' as the *logos*, that which asserts the meaningfulness of life, and that which determines the elements being and non-being in both an ideal and real sense. Even the absence of the definite article in the phrase 'ultimate concern' is meant to reinforce both its intimate character and the impossibility of humanity escaping it.[40]

The initially abstract nature of the concept of ultimate concern also serves to distinguish it from 'preliminary' concern. Preliminary concern is an attitude of indifference to what is ultimate and is manifest as relativism or idolatry – the elevation of what is finite to the level of ultimate, or an attitude of indifference to what is ultimate.[41] Problems arise in theology both when the situation is elevated above the message, and when the message does not take adequate account of the context of its transmission. Tillich's attempted repair of these twin problems compels his own system and informs his critique of historical and contemporary theological approaches.

This general discussion of ultimate concern and the problems facing humanity provides a background for Tillich's more specific, problem-focused approach to theology. In the introduction of the *Systematic Theology*, Tillich defines theology in terms of what it should not be. He articulates what he thinks are the main problems facing twentieth-century theology by offering critiques of three approaches to theology against which he positions his apologetic theology: the kerygmatic, the natural and the logical.[42]

First, Tillich is concerned with what he calls a supranaturalistic approach in which the absoluteness of the *kerygma*, or 'message' of revelation, obscures the 'situation' in which it occurs and the human situation to which it is directed. Though Tillich does not attach any names to supranaturalism, he is likely thinking again of Barth. Evidence of this comes earlier in the introduction to the *Systematic Theology*, where Tillich refers to Barth's theology as kerygmatic, by which he means that the 'unchangeable truth' of the Christian message is asserted 'over' the changing demands of the human situation rather than seeing revelation as involving human participation in, or at least reception of, revelation.[43]

The consequences of supranaturalism include a dichotomy between revelation and the world, or message and situation, and a devaluing of human experience and thought in the face of divine transcendence. The division of revelation from the experience of it, as though divine truth simply falls into a corrupted world, results in two theological approaches: orthodoxy and fundamentalism. Tillich claims that the former emphasizes the unchangeable nature of eternal truth in confessional statements that stultify theology, while the latter tends to exalt the past as 'an unchangeable message against the theological truth of today and tomorrow'.[44] Tillich also condemns a form of fundamentalism that he calls 'biblicism', an approach that avoids philosophical terminology in a futile effort to deliver a 'pure' message. The folly is twofold. First, philosophy has always influenced Christian doctrine and confession. Second,

The Bible itself always uses the categories and concepts which describe the structure of experience. On every page of every religious or theological text these concepts appear: time, space, cause, thing, subject, nature, movement, freedom, necessity, value, knowledge, experience, being and not-being.[45]

Supranaturalism, and the related approaches of orthodoxy, fundamentalism and biblicism, make faith irrational and unhistorical. In all, theology is made static by simplifying and elevating Scripture itself to an extent which denies both its interaction with other thought processes and the diversity of thought present in Scripture itself.

Second, Tillich is concerned with a naturalism caused by romanticizing the human condition, or exalting the power of human cognition. This can be the result either of *situation* overwhelming *message*, or of situation and message being confused. His targets here include Spinozistic pantheism, as well as natural theology and the false hope of Christian socialism. In this case also Tillich does not identify his critique with particular people. He does, however, distinguish naturalism from the reasoned argumentation for the existence of God, which he calls dualism, and which is addressed below. Tillich also groups natural theology and religious socialism together as attempts to reduce the vision of kerygma to a practical or moral utopia, thereby negating the transcendent vision of the kerygma.[46]

Finally, Tillich is concerned with what he calls dualistic theology. Though briefly, Tillich characterizes dualism as the approach to revelation according to rigid categories of argument.[47] Dualism places theology within closed systems of argument and is therefore distinct from naturalism, pantheism and vitalism, which reduce God to what is worldly. Tillich's clearest comment on this subject comes later in the first volume of the *Systematic Theology*:

> The task of a theological treatment of the traditional arguments for the existence of God is twofold: to develop the question of God which they express and to expose the impotency of the 'arguments', their inability to answer the question of God. These arguments bring the ontological analysis to a conclusion by disclosing that the question of God is implied in the finite structure of being. In performing this function, they partially accept and also partially reject traditional natural theology, and they drive reason to the quest for revelation.[48]

Theology, for Tillich, is an attempt to describe the conflicts of human existence and the resolution of them that occurs through revelation.

'[Theology] answers the questions implied in the "situation" in the power of the eternal message and with the means provided by the situation whose questions it answers.'[49] Good theology has a responsibility to portray revelation neither as completely inaccessible, nor as accessible only through nature and/or argumentation.

Whether its emphasis is kerygmatic, natural or logical, a theological approach, for Tillich, is insufficient when its focus becomes too narrow. Despite criticisms indicating the contrary,[50] this includes natural theology, which emphasizes the centrality of immanent human experience to the exclusion of the transcendence of revelation. As is clear in his early article criticizing Barth's use of dialectic, for Tillich, all theology, by virtue of being a human endeavour, is theology 'from below'. However, he does not want the extreme estrangement of the human situation to be tragically exalted. This concern has an epistemological correlate: the reduction of cognition either to abstraction or to empiricism.[51] Both are limited by a one-sided emphasis on the basis of knowledge as either subjective or objective. Thus, Tillich proposes that existence is 'encounter'; that is, the mutual participation of subject and object, which is reflected in the act of cognition.

Humanity must be capable of interacting with revelation, if only to know that what it takes *as* revelation *is* revealed, and not something which has bubbled up out of the conflicts, both cognitive and existential, of human life. Tillich does say that 'Man is the question he asks about himself, before a question is formulated.'[52] However, Tillich also states that 'The existential question, namely, man himself in the conflicts of his existential situation, is not the source for the revelatory answer formulated by theology.'[53] Later, Tillich emphasizes that 'If God were not also in man so that man could ask for God, God's speaking to man could not be perceived by man.'[54] The aim of Tillich's system is to maintain the ontological priority of the 'answer', or revelation, while maintaining the apologetic priority of the 'the question man asks about himself'.[55]

This prompts a question: If the aim of an apologetic, or answering, theology is to frame the revelatory answers to existential questions, what is the role of philosophy in the process of formulating the questions themselves? Though its definition depends on its contextual use, philosophy is generally concerned, says Tillich, with categories, structural laws and universal concepts.[56] While theology studies the meaning of being, philosophy is the study of the structures of being.[57] As a method of analysing existence, philosophy tends to formalize and objectify. But because it analyses the human condition and expresses the experience of being and cognition, philosophy is somehow involved in the theological task. Philosophy is also foremost among all disciplines related to theology, for Tillich, because 'the analysis of the human situation is done in terms which today are called "existential"'.[58]

The aim of correlation is to relate 'questions implied in the situation with the answers implied in the message'.[59] Therefore, theology is responsible for the 'answers implied in the message', because by 'message' Tillich means the symbols of revelation: God as Creator, Christ and Spirit. Because Tillich says that philosophy 'asks questions' about the nature of existence and thought and their relation, it could easily be interpreted that philosophy as a discipline is responsible for formulating the questions 'implied in the [existential] situation'. However, Tillich does not intend for theology and philosophy to perform such tasks, in a way mutually exclusive of each other, in the *Systematic Theology*.

Tillich asks, 'What is the relation between the ontological question of the philosopher and of the theologian?'[60] He suggests that theology and philosophy share the same object of concern, the *logos* and therefore are asking questions about the same thing when they ask questions about thought and existence. While he does say that apologetic theology is methodologically responsible for answering the questions implied in the situation of existence, Tillich does not say that philosophy alone is methodologically responsible for asking those questions. There is a difference between saying that philosophy asks ontological questions and giving philosophy the methodological responsibility to do so within a theological system. 'Philosophy necessarily asks the question of reality as a whole, the question of the structure of being. Theology necessarily asks the same question, for that which concerns us ultimately belongs to reality as a whole; it must belong to being.'[61] Existential philosophy does ask questions about reality as a whole, about the structures of being, but so does theology.[62]

The passage most frequently cited to support the argument that Tillich considers philosophy to be entirely responsible for posing the questions of existence comes from the second volume of the *Systematic Theology*. Here Tillich says that to be correlated implies that existential questions and theological answers are independent of each other, but that question and answer also imply 'mutual dependence'.[63]

This statement, however, occurs within the context of a discussion of the problem of natural theology. In affirming the independence and interdependence of 'question and answer' Tillich is referring to the independence and interdependence of existence and revelation. His argument is that the infinite truth that theology attempts to express is related to human finitude, but cannot be derived from it. The discussion here is not about the roles and relationship of philosophy and theology, but about the limitations of natural theology.

The marginalization of philosophy in the *Systematic Theology* does not mean that philosophy, for Tillich, is incapable of asking existential questions. Theology and philosophy are united in asking 'the question of being',[64] what it means to be, to speak, to create, to know. There are no duplicate worlds: a real world, the province of philosophy, and a transcendent world, the province of theology.[65] Both disciplines serve the one *logos*:

> The Christian claim that the *logos* who has become concrete in Jesus as the Christ is at the same time the universal *logos* includes the claim that wherever the *logos* is at work it agrees with the Christian message. No philosophy which is obedient to the universal *logos* can contradict the concrete *logos*, the *Logos* 'who became flesh'.[66]

There are not two worlds built upon each other, as either a theological or philosophical dualism would suggest. Rather, theology and philosophy represent two general approaches to the question of existence.

What responsibility, then, does Tillich assign philosophy in the *Systematic Theology*? In the introduction to the system Tillich first describes philosophy as a 'conceptual tool'.[67] Here, Tillich makes the subordination of philosophy to theology clear: 'Theology formulates the questions implied in human existence, and theology formulates the answers implied in divine self-manifestation under the guidance of the questions implied in human existence.'[68] Theology is responsible for both the questions and answers of existence, while philosophy is relegated to a group including many other disciplines whose contribution theology organizes:

> The analysis of the human situation employs materials made available by man's creative self-interpretation in all realms of culture. Philosophy contributes, but so do poetry, drama, the novel,

therapeutic psychology, and sociology. The theologian organizes these materials in relation to the answer given by the Christian message.[69]

Philosophy is characterized here as an empirical science. The philosopher tries to maintain 'detached objectivity toward being and structures', with a passion 'only for truth, not for the personal'.[70] In contrast, the theologian is 'involved with his object' and is concerned with the 'meaning of existence', not the 'structure of existence' only.[71] The weakness of such distinctions is readily apparent, not least because Tillich elsewhere says that the object of philosophical investigation is the same *logos* as that of theology.

Although he acknowledges that there are many different kinds of philosophy, Tillich's inventory falls within two categories: natural idealism and logical positivism. The conflation of idealism and naturalism is the result of Tillich's narrow definition of their common origination in an experience of a 'mystical *a priori*'.[72] When philosophy is not naturalism or the 'epistemology and ethics' which he identifies with 'the neo-Kantians' of the nineteenth century, it is 'logical positivism', with which no one is identified.[73] These caricatures of idealism and positivism are never explained by Tillich and, even together, fall far short of an adequate definition of philosophy. Philosophy is plainly as concerned with the meaning of existence as is theology.[74] Tillich's overly empirical characterization of philosophy seems to confuse the desired precision of philosophical investigation with the precision sought in scientific testing.[75]

The distinction between theology and philosophy, however, is not necessarily their object, but what constitutes an authoritative account of their object. For example, although Tillich argues that theology and philosophy share the same object of concern, the *logos*, he says that the philosopher and the theologian don't stand in opposition because they share no common ground – no synthesis is possible. By 'no common ground' Tillich could mean one of two things. First, the lack of common ground could refer to a disparity of authority, between theology and philosophy, in relation to the *logos*. Revelation does not contradict or supersede reason, but the theologian is committed to accepting revelation as authoritative while the philosopher is not.[76] Second, the denial of common ground could be linked to Tillich's suspicion of what he calls the 'dream of a

"Christian philosophy"'. Tillich is wary of subjecting the meaning of revelation to an authority other than the universal *logos* itself, for example the data of historical research, a particular theologian or philosopher or ecclesial authority.[77] A Christian philosophy would also problematically subjugate philosophy to theological concerns. Tillich's suspicion of the synthesis of theology and philosophy is not just on behalf of theology, but also on behalf of philosophy. Neither discipline can be a corrective for the other since each claims authority in different ways and from different sources.

There are significant problems with Tillich's definition of philosophy in the introduction of the *Systematic Theology*. One problem is that Tillich presents an overly narrow definition of philosophy. Another problem with Tillich's definition of philosophy can be addressed from within his own system. It has to do with the concept of the *logos*, which can and does mean many different things. Tillich makes a distinction between the 'universal *logos*' and the 'concrete *logos*' only to identify them as the non-contradictory objects of philosophy and theology respectively. Yet, even if theology and philosophy are merely giving different names to the same thing when they discuss the *logos*, Tillich's concept of 'ultimate concern' clearly suggests that theology has a claim to something more. As a result, philosophy becomes a handmaid to theology.[78]

The *Systematic Theology* is devoted to demonstrating how the 'symbols' of Christianity provide answers to the questions that result from existence; and revelation's primary symbol is what Tillich calls the 'Christian *logos*', that is, Christ, the New Being. Yet, he also asserts that this concrete or revealed *logos* is the same as the universal *logos* of philosophy, and that revelation is not new information.[79] The question is, if theology and philosophy have the same object of investigation, what is the *something more* to which theology has access?

One possible response is that, in taking the experience of revelation as *authoritative*, theology contributes a different awareness of existence from what other disciplines propose. More specifically, theology and philosophy do not offer competing accounts of existence and experience, but different criteria for what constitutes the data of experience. For example, Tillich refers to cosmological arguments not as answers, but as statements of the question of existence. What philosophy means by transcendence, that is self-consciousness, is not what theology means by transcendence, that is divinity. The 'something more' of Tillich's theological framing of the questions of existence is the anticipation of religious experience as constitutive of the human experience, an assumption that may or may not appeal to the philosopher. In sum, Tillich does not think that he is correlating two different facts, methods or approaches when he claims to correlate theology and philosophy, but that he is relating the experience of reality that takes Christian scripture and its historical and theological symbols as authoritative, with that experience which does not.

Another possible response is to say that theology does not contribute anything *more* than philosophy, but that the theology in which Tillich is engaging, because it attempts to include the analysis of both theology and philosophy, is of a different order than other philosophical or theological discussions. Borrowing a concept of Tillich's early writings, one commentator suggests that 'first-order thought', or cognition, is directed towards reality, or experience, while 'second-order thought', or reflection, is directed at first-order thought. 'In philosophy, the mind grasps reality as such; in religious cognition (theology), the mind is grasped by reality as such. In second-order thought, the mind relates its acts of grasping reality and of being grasped by reality.'[80] For religious cognition, the language of symbol may not be very helpful, as it implies something beyond the experience in an unreflective way. Reflection, however, intentionally relates the experience of grasping or being grasped to something else, especially other experiences.

The terminology of formally 'correlating' theology and philosophy can be slightly misleading because it implies a formal equation of two sets of data, rather than expanding the legitimating terms of what counts as experience and how to relate it. Tillich's many distinctions compound this difficulty, especially the distinctions between universal *logos* and concrete *logos*, and question and answer. The tendency to reduce philosophy to either idealism or positivism in the *Systematic Theology* severely limits even the possible contribution of philosophy. However, correlation suggests that Tillich sets two related tasks for the *Systematic Theology*. The first is to have theology and philosophy ask questions regarding human existence. The second is to demonstrate that the symbols of the Christian religion provide the appropriate response. The theologian's location of authority in the experience of revelation grounds his bias towards a Christian theological account of human existence. The method of correlation functions not so much as correlation of autonomous philosophical questions and heteronomous theological answers, but as the 'elevation' of inherently religious ideas of estrangement (sin) and reconciliation (salvation), into the framework of Christian theology.[81]

PART II

'ANSWERING' THEOLOGY: QUESTIONS OF EXISTENCE AND PROBLEMS OF THEOLOGY

CHAPTER THREE

BEING AND GOD

Tillich's typology of kerygmatic 'message' and human 'situation' establishes the need for theology to answer the questions posed by existence. Through the concept of being-itself, he demonstrates the underlying connection between the divine and the human, the 'essential' balance and 'existential' imbalance of the universal concepts of being and non-being. However, the correlation of theological symbols and philosophical concepts is not merely an attempt to transpose theology into a different idiom. It is an attempt to clarify the meaning of revelation for the human situation, which in the nineteenth and twentieth centuries is most frequently expressed in ontological and existential terms. Because, as a human endeavour, theology is prone to ambiguity, Tillich's task in the *Systematic Theology* is not only to make theology relevant to the present age, but also to repair some of the problems that he thinks make theology irrelevant to that age.

As a result, the *Systematic Theology* must not be read only as a correlative theology, but also as Tillich's response to problems he believes contemporary theology faces. Three central concerns provide the structure of the system: the necessity of an actualized God for human existence; the restatement of Christology in terms of the human condition of estrangement and the sins of self-elevation; and the notion of the Spiritual Presence within, but also as a critique of, the Spiritual Community. In his system, Tillich relates an aspect of existence with a person of the triune God: 'Being' with 'God'; 'Existence' with 'the Christ'; and the 'Spiritual Community' with the Spirit, or the 'Spiritual Presence'. In each section of the system, Tillich offers a repair of the problem he identifies in each doctrine. In this chapter, we will consider the doctrines of God, Christ and Spirit, primarily as articulated in the *Systematic Theology*, in light of the theological problems they address.

Tillich describes 'God' as a religious and cultural symbol that can only partially describe the ultimate meaning to which it refers. As a symbol, the word 'God' is only a mediating expression of the human knowledge of revelation. Tillich often employs the term the 'Unconditioned', by which he means the infinitely powerful ground of meaning and being without the imposed categories of human understanding.[1] It is an ideal concept, a pre-cognitive and objective power, or potential, which manifests itself and thereby receives description through the medium of human experience. This concept of God and Being owes much to Schelling's later philosophy of God as an infinitely potential power that 'becomes' through its own externalizing nature.[2]

Tillich's theology is often formulated in response to other theologies with which he disagrees. In the case of the Unconditioned, Tillich is responding to theologies which either remove God from the human perspective altogether, or reduce God to 'a being' alongside other beings.[3] The language of the Unconditioned acknowledges the infinity of God and the necessarily finite human knowledge of God, but still permits logical reference for the sake of understanding. Biblical and theological concepts of God are not dispensed with, rather, they stand alongside this more philosophical concept to allow Tillich to address problems he perceives in contemporary theology. Whether this is a successful or necessary enterprise continues to be debated.

In the *Systematic Theology*, the place of the Unconditioned in human existence and cognition is more carefully articulated in the typology of being, non-being and being-itself.[4] Being-itself, or 'the power of being-itself', is the power of God, discernable in the Creation of God, the revelation of Jesus the Christ, and the Spiritual Presence within human life and history. However, as revealed power, being-itself comprises two impulses: 'being', the impulse to create, to reveal, to be present; and 'non-being', the necessary limitation of that infinite potential. This duality of being and non-being is *the* ontological concept of Tillich's theology and forms the basis of both his doctrine of God and his anthropology.

ONTOLOGY IN THE *SYSTEMATIC THEOLOGY*

Ontology and reason

Before giving an ontological account of revelation, according to Tillich, 'theology must give a description of cognitive reason under the conditions of existence.'[5] In the first section of the *Systematic Theology*,

'Reason and Revelation', Tillich describes human reason as dialectically structured; that is, as best described by two opposing, but
equally necessary elements. In cognition, this polarity can be observed
in three pairs of inclinations: autonomy and heteronomy, relativism
and absolutism and formalism and emotionalism.[6] In each, Tillich
argues that the claim of reason to be blindly self-critical must be
replaced with an approach to reason which is self-critical *in light of*
revelation. To do so, he demonstrates that the competitive, dialectical
inclinations of reason can be resolved when reason is 'reunited with
its depth', which is revelation. This approach to reason exposes the
fundamentally ontological nature of his system. The criteria of what
is authoritative for human cognition ultimately rests in the human
experience of the revelation of being-itself. For Tillich, epistemology
is the knowledge of 'knowing', while ontology is the knowledge of
'being'. However, this also implies that 'epistemology is part of ontology, for knowing is an event within the totality of events'.[7] For Tillich,
every epistemological assertion is implicitly ontological. However,
Tillich has not arrived at this concept of reason without precedent.

Because human reason is finite, it, like existence itself, is subject to
the conflicted 'conditions of existence'. He identifies the historical
conflict inherent in discourse on reason as being between two competing concepts. The first is an 'ontological' concept, or a 'classical
concept', an organic approach he associates largely with Plato and
which he characterizes as operative in cognitive, aesthetic, practical,
emotional and technical functions of the human mind. The second
concept of reason he calls the 'technical concept', which he associates most closely with the English empiricist reaction to German
Idealism. The latter concept of reason as the mere capacity for cognition, closely aligned to logic, is distinctly narrow.[8] However, the distinction between ontological and technical reason is meant to
demonstrate two different relationships of cognition to revelation.

Technical reason seeks control over the knowledge of revelation,
while ontological, or 'ecstatic reason', is 'grasped' by revelation, causing reason to 'seek union' with the source of revelation.[9] By means of
the first, an object is grasped by the subject and controlled. By means
of the second, a subject is grasped by its object, and compelled. According to Tillich, theology needs both approaches. The technical concept
of reason does help to organize and systematize. However, ontological reason is a term Tillich favours in order to expand the definition
of reason in two respects. First, for ontological reason all aspects

of existence, not just the cognitive, are informative. Second, the presence of reason in everything suggests a common creative source of both cognition and being, which Tillich calls 'depth'.[10]

Within existence, this depth, or 'purity of reason', is fallen.[11] As we have seen, this is behind Tillich's insistence that theology can only refer to its experience of revelation symbolically because, in its fallen state, the human experience of truth is finite and limited.[12] In theological terms, history stands between the fall from perfect 'potential', the Garden of Eden, and complete fulfilment or actualization of potential, called the Kingdom of God. Between these moments, in the 'flux of time', reason exists only 'fragmentarily' and is, therefore, subject to the polarized conflict of inclinations listed above. These polarities are meant, however, not to be absolute categories, but polar spectra that characterizze all human reason. As a description of a logical relationship, elements within each polarity are inseparable. Yet, for Tillich, the act of knowing is both an act of union, in which the gap between subject and object is overcome, and an act of detachment, in which subject and object acknowledge their difference. As simultaneous acts of distinction and identity, however, cognition expresses an inclination towards unity.

Because of the eternal division and conflict of human cognition, represented by the polar categories of reason and its finitude, human reason on its own is incapable of achieving the unity it seeks. For Tillich, the answer to the existential quest for unity of subject and object is the ecstatic, that is 'grasping', experience of revelation. Revelation is manifest as mystery, ecstasy and sign-event, or miracle.[13] Mystery is a dimension which precedes the subject–object relationship. Ecstasy is a condition in which the mind is grasped and transcends the experience of the threat of non-being. Miracle is an astonishing sign which can be manifest within the rational structure of reality, and yet preserve the structure and meaning of reality. Revelation is capable of speaking through history: through individuals and groups. As Word, revelation is not like ordinary language, nor is it the transmission of knowledge. Rather, revelation is the experience of mystery and the transmission of truth, which is expressed in Christian symbols.

Despite the transcendent nature of revelation, Tillich emphasizes that revelation occurs within history. Yet, in order to both grasp reason and convey a truth transcendent of finite existence, revelation must be able to sacrifice the particularity of its manifestation. Put another way, the conflicts of finite cognition and existence can only be overcome by a finite revelation of the infinite that is also capable of transcending its finite form. Revelation is said to judge religion, culture, history and reason, because it ultimately sacrifices its conditioned manifestation to its Unconditioned truth.[14] In subsequent chapters we will see that, for Tillich, the self-negation characteristic of revelation is most enduringly present in Jesus as the Christ and the symbol of the Cross. Revelation as the Christ both accomplishes and displays the unity characteristic of divinity, but in human existence. In self-negation, revelation ultimately unifies what is universal and concrete by sacrificing concrete form to universal meaning. For now, it is important to observe that Tillich describes revelation as 'grasping' the conflicts of reason, in order to repair reason which, left to its own conflicted state, would not be capable of expressing anything beyond the finite.

Ontology and revelation

In 'Reason and Revelation', Tillich describes the conflicts of human reason in such a way that revelation can be described as the source of their resolution. In the second section of the *Systematic Theology*, 'Being and God', Tillich describes the conflicts endemic to human existence in order to do the same. At the most basic level, Tillich defines being as the inclination to take form and non-being as the inclination to resist taking form. In uncreated essence, these inclinations or forces are equal, opposed and held in unity. In existence, they are no longer united, but estranged, and are therefore the cause of conflict and ambiguity.

Non-being, says Tillich, is the 'not-yet' and 'no more' of being, by which he means the limitation of otherwise unlimited being.[15] He calls this polarity 'dialectical', so that the non-being he defines as the dialectical counterpart of being is different from the non-dialectical *nihil*, or ουκ ov, out of which God created.[16] Tillich makes this distinction because historically, he says, a problem results when Christianity conceives of non-being dialectically. The presence of evil in the world raises the question of the origin of evil. If, however, there is no original source of being other than God, who is good, there is no place to locate, even in principle, the origin of evil or non-being, but in God. Tillich variously associates such a compromise with

Böhme's *Ungrund*, Schelling's first potency, and Hegel's notion of antithesis.[17]

Against these notions of non-being, which maintain the logical priority of non-being, Tillich asserts the ontological priority of being. As support for this assertion he offers a semantic argument – that, without being, a concept of non-being is meaningless. However, Tillich also associates the relationship of non-being and being through a historical account of sin. He says that, for Augustine, the idea that sin is non-being does not suggest that sin has no reality, but that as non-being resists being, so sin is a perversion of being. Tillich's primary concern, however, is to show the link between the divine balance of being and non-being, and the human imbalance of these elements. The limitation of potential being into actualized human form is unintelligible without a concept of dialectical non-being.[18]

Being and non-being are essentially equal and opposing inclinations whose imbalance in existence causes the conflicts of human existence. For Tillich, however, there are also three things endemic to all human existence: prescribed, finite limitations; an inner *telos* that guides the process of becoming; and the creative capacity for imaginative transcendence.[19] Humanity, relative to the animal kingdom, is uniquely aware of its place within a self-world relationship. The designation 'self', for Tillich, is not just 'ego', but 'self-conscious ego'.[20] Humanity is aware of the reality of being and the possibility of not-being, and of finitude and the possible transcendence of it, or infinity. As we have seen, this awareness is the result of the ontological connection between essence and existence. This awareness, because it occurs within existence, is the source not only of anxiety, but also of the desire for transcendence.

The ontological polarity of being and non-being in this section of the system is related to the subject–object structure of reason in the previous section. However, because Tillich eventually uses the essential polarity of being and non-being to describe God, he is careful to clarify what this polarity entails. Like the self-world awareness of existence, the subject–object structure of cognition prevents either element from being derived from the other. Of course, objectification is natural. 'In the cognitive realm everything toward which the cognitive act is directed is considered an object, be it God or a stone, be it one's self or a mathematical definition.'[21] Tillich cautions that God cannot be included in the subject–object scheme in such a way as to become an object alongside others. Otherwise, God ceases to be the 'ground of being', or the God who is really God, and becomes merely an object alongside other objects.

The tension of existence, in both the self-world and subject-object structures, is manifest in what Tillich calls the 'ontological elements', or polarities: individualization and participation, dynamics and form, and freedom and destiny.[22] Each results from the mixture of being and non-being under the conditions of existence, and each has a dialectical structure. In respect to the first polarity, the individual is both singular and a participant in an environment. Individuals dialectically participate in a community of other individuals through 'union' and through 'resistance', which are expressive of a universal *telos*.

In respect to the second polarity, existence, or 'being something', implies form. Yet, 'Every form forms something. The question is: What is this "something"? We have called it dynamics.'[23] In contrast to the concretising inclination of form 'to be', dynamics appears as the power of non-being. Tillich associates dynamics variously with Böhme's *Urgrund*, Schopenhauer's *will*, Freud's *unconscious*, and with mythological concepts such as chaos, the *tohu-va-bohu*, the night, the emptiness and the *nihil* which precedes creation.[24]

In respect to the third polarity, 'Freedom is experienced as deliberation, decision and responsibility', that is, of weighing, excluding and accounting for choices.[25] Destiny, not the traditional 'necessity', is the counterpart in this polarity. For Tillich, destiny is neither a Greek notion of fate, nor does it refer to something anticipated and yet unchangeable. Destiny is 'that out of which our decisions arise . . . the concreteness of our being which makes all our decisions *our* decisions'.[26] Destiny is the basis for free decision making, which in turn further shapes one's destiny.

To these polarities under the conditions of existence, revelation comes in the form of God as being-itself, or 'the power of being-itself'.[27] In the same way that Tillich describes a general notion of revelation as the power of reconciliation for conflicted reason, the revelation of God as 'being-itself' provides reconciliation of conflicted existence. As being-itself, God is the source of all dynamic substance and form, yet is beyond both essence and existence, beyond mere potential and everything actual.[28] God is the name given to the source of dynamics, yet God is also actual only through that which is concrete. Though transcendent of the division of subject and object, God participates, fulfilling the quest of individuals and communities. At once, God sets and transcends the limits of existence, providing finite freedom and destiny by originating, sustaining and directing all creativity and life.[29]

In this section of the *Systematic Theology*, Tillich describes human existence as rooted in divine essence. As being-itself, God constitutes the power of being and non-being for human existence as well as for Godself. What is balanced in God, however, is unbalanced in humanity. Under the 'conditions of existence', the polarity of being and non-being creates conflict in human existence. Because being and non-being are constitutive of both divine essence and human existence, and because of the unique human capacity for self-consciousness that Tillich takes as given, human existence, though conflicted, is aware of the possibility of transcending that conflict. However, because of its finitude, humanity is ultimately incapable of transcendence on its own.

The only possible hope of reconciliation of conflicted existence resides in being-itself, or the source of polarity: God. This does not mean that revelation as being-itself is a merely logical answer to the conflicts of existence caused by the polarity of being and non-being. Rather, the human experience of polarity, knowledge of being and non-being, and awareness of the absence of their reconciliation, causes anxiety. As the only answer to this anxiety, Tillich suggests that revelation does not merely happen to humanity, but that humanity desires revelation. However, Tillich does not make clear the extent to which humanity knows precisely what it desires. Anxiety merely forms the 'question of existence'.[30]

BEING AND ANXIETY IN *THE COURAGE TO BE*

Occasionally, in the *Systematic Theology*, Tillich uses the term 'anxiety' to describe the infinite possibility of non-being, and 'courage' to describe the definitive human quest for revelation characteristic of the infinite creativity of being.[31] Used this way, the concepts of being and non-being enable Tillich to portray the connection between perfectly balanced being-itself and the imbalance characteristic of human existence. Anxiety and courage, however, imply something more than primary forces or possibility; they describe the effect of these forces present in the human condition.

In *The Courage To Be*, first published one year after the first volume of the *Systematic Theology*, Tillich provides a more existential discussion of anxiety and courage. Anxiety refers to the object-less fear of non-existence, either as death, meaninglessness, or condemnation. For Tillich, anxiety is a natural state of being for a human creature capable of conceiving of its own existence. The concept of being leads to the inevitable human question of the radical possibility of non-being, and the various ways in which non-being is present in existence. Courage, however, refers to human 'self-affirmation "in-spite-of" . . . that which tends to prevent the self from affirming itself'.[32] In other words, while humanity is capable of considering the possibility that it *might not have been*, and that it will eventually *not be*, it is nonetheless capable of vitality in the face of inevitable existential anxiety. Tillich describes this 'courage to be' in terms of three kinds of human activity: participation, individualization and transcendence. These terms are central to Tillich's later systematic description of the place of human agency within the history of salvation, or 'essentialization'.

Every human activity is also both an action of the individual and an action that takes place within a context – what Tillich calls the polarity of 'self and world'.[33] There is a necessary distinction to be drawn between the self and its environment, but they are 'polar' for Tillich because the possibility of distinguishing a 'self' implies an environment or an 'other' from which the self can distinguish itself. The concept of self and world helps Tillich describe courage in human life as the activities of participation and individualization.

In the concept of participation, the human self is both part of something and different from it. As an individual participates in relationship, in groups and in the physical environment, each experience necessarily gives him more definition – he 'becomes' who he is. At the same time, in more clearly defining himself 'as' an individual, the human self also distinguishes, more clearly, what he is not – in choosing who he is, he determines who he is not. Thus, the activity of 'participating' in life is simultaneously an act of discovery and loss. Thus, the courage to be, in the activity of participation, is the 'courage to be a part' only,[34] to define oneself both in terms of what one is and what one is not. Tillich identifies this conceptual development of participatory self-definition with the socio-political concepts of primitive collectivism, medieval semi-collectivism and democratic conformity.[35] This historical perspective of the development of participation moves from being *merely* a part of a group to being in *harmony* with the group, to being a *free* member of a group.

Individualization is the activity of the self which, having undergone definition by the process of participation, seeks to focus only on what one is. If the activity of participation involves both self and world, individualization is the activity that focuses on the self. Tillich beings by identifying Bohemianism, Romanticism and Naturalism as movements that contributed to the development of a radical, though not necessarily irrational, individualism. Not without consideration for the world, but viewing everything, including the world, from the position of the self, individualization is most clearly expressed in the 'attitude', or approach, of existentialism. Tillich distinguishes the inclusive and organic 'existential attitude' from formal Existentialism, which he defines as a philosophical theory with a specific, often exclusively cognitive, theoretical and detached content, and which he associates mostly with Hegel.[36] Nonetheless, despite its organic and increasingly artistic expressions, individualization in the form of existentialism's focus on the individual as free and autonomous has also yielded a definitive despair about the human condition. Even the boundless creativity and vitality of humanity cannot overcome the obdurate limitations of existence, especially the unavoidable fate of death.

Expressed in the human activities of participation and individualization, the concept of courage develops strength and diversity, but does not yet attain a description of limitlessness that allows it to be an adequate response to anxiety. Within the polarity of self and world there can be an assertion of courage, but not courage enough to answer the questions of doubt, fear and despair characteristic of existence. The final description of the courage to be, therefore, must account for a power that is greater than death, meaninglessness and condemnation. For Tillich, this is the power of being-itself which, as we have already seen, transcends the inclinations of being and non-being because it is the balanced unity of the two.

Religion, says Tillich, 'is the state of being grasped by the power of being itself'.[37] Being-itself is experienced in three ways: as mystical experiences of the divine which are mediated through the world; as revelation which is threatened neither by the loss of the world nor of oneself, and is in this way unmediated; and as the acceptance of justification despite guilt, 'the courage to accept acceptance'.[38] Of this kind of courage, says Tillich, 'it is not the good or the wise or the pious who are entitled to the courage to accept acceptance but those who are lacking in all these qualities and are aware of being unacceptable'.[39] The power of being-itself, because it is unbounded by the limitations of existence, is the source of courage for all humanity. Thus, the courage to be that can overcome anxiety, fear and death, is found in that which transcends the imbalance of being and non-being characteristic of human existence: God.

ADDRESSING THE NEED FOR AN ACTUALIZING GOD

As we have seen, Tillich often refers to God as 'the power of being', 'the power of being-itself' or simply as 'being-itself'. According to Tillich, this conceptualization is necessary in order to describe the unique way in which God is the ground of all being, while avoiding both overly abstract and overly personal concepts of God. This results in two major steps in Tillich's doctrine of God: replacing ontological proofs for the existence of God with a new concept of infinity and describing God as 'living'.

The main value of traditional ontological proofs for the existence of God, according to Tillich, is that they acknowledge an unconditional element in the structure and reason of reality.[40] The usefulness of ontological proofs is limited, however, to representing the 'question of God'. The ontological conceptualization of God can guarantee the potential of human awareness of God, but not God *as* God. Arguments that try to join 'being' to the guarantee of awareness can only 'pervert insight'. For example, according to Tillich, Anselm's concept of God as a necessary thought is valid for thinking, as it 'implies an unconditional element which transcends objectivity and subjectivity'.[41] In this case, the concept of God is a logical guarantor of the possibility of thought about God. However, the concept is not adequate as a guarantor of being, because the *existence* of a being is not implied in the *concept* of a highest being.[42]

Tillich's discussion of ontological proofs is not, however, primarily concerned with engaging scholastic theology, but with more general theological problems. In addressing issues of historically 'ontological' theology, Tillich is targeting problems that he identifies with overly rationalistic approaches to theology: pantheism, theism and deism. In this context, Tillich presents a new concept of infinity, which he defines not as quantity but as quality; not as entity, but as power. Defining infinity as a quality of being-itself, Tillich can describe God as 'calling' human existential being to reunification with being-itself. The notion of a 'substance' that grounds the 'persons' of God is replaced with the concept of the 'power' of the living God, or of being-itself that 'grasps' finite reason and existence through the revelation of infinite possibility.

For Tillich, finitude is not exactly equal to existence, and infinity is not exactly equal to essence. Rather, finitude is the existent being's cognitive awareness of limitation, and infinity is the possibility of unlimited transcendence. The possibility of transcendence is not the same as being-itself, but is a directive issued by it.[43] Finite humanity is capable of self-transcendence not because of an infinite being, but because of unlimited potential, issued by being-itself in revelation. Infinity is a quality of, not simply an unlimited quantity of, essence and power. The 'power' of divine essence, as infinity, is the capacity to hold being and non-being in balance, to be both actual and potential, and to provide the foundation of creation, life and the living relationship between humanity and divinity. As a quality and not a quantity, infinity is an expression of the power by which humanity is called to essentialization: the 'power' of the Christ as New Being and of the Spiritual Presence.

Infinity is an early conceptual description of how being-itself, or undisrupted essence, can both reach and transcend finitude. Tillich considers the divine 'call' to infinity to be expressive of humanity's belonging to that which is beyond the existential imbalance of being and non-being, namely, being-itself.[44] Once being-itself is revealed to humanity, humanity can conceive of, though not exhaustively, that to which it transcends. The possibility of self-transcendence is enough, for Tillich, to reinforce a positive connection between being and being-itself.

The concept of infinity, then, is as useful as a traditional ontological proof insofar as it points to the potentially limitless transcendence of cognitive awareness. Conceptually, however, infinity is as limited as that proof because it cannot guarantee the existence of a highest being. This, however, is a reality Tillich acknowledges. In Tillich's language, ontological proofs can only pose the 'question of God', or describe the potential transcendence of cognitive awareness. Cosmological proofs have a similar function for Tillich. The positing of a 'first cause' is one possible starting point in a logical argument, but does not provide proof of a 'being' which initiates a causal chain. That is to say, the logical need for an unmoved mover does not guarantee its existence. Even the teleological argument for the necessity of an unthreatened 'meaning' of life, or *telos*, cannot guarantee the existence of such an infinite meaning.[45]

The discussion of infinity is only part of a larger effort to allow Tillich to describe God as living, creating and relating. God as 'living' addresses the existential concern of his system: that the transcendent God who is said to reveal is also inherently connected to the humanity to which God reveals. In response to theologies which emphasize the transcendence of God as a being completely distinct from humanity, Tillich emphasizes that human life is an intimate part of the life of God.

As the power of being-itself, God in all three persons is the ground of all being. Tillich calls the process of the continual actualization of this ground the 'life of God', where life is 'the process in which potential being becomes actual being . . . the actualization of the structural elements of being in their unity and in their tension'.[46] As parts of a continual process the impulses to remain as pure potentiality and to be actualized are always in tension. However, 'in God there is no distinction between potentiality and actuality'.[47] The polar elements are rooted in the divine life, in the distinction of being and non-being, but the divine life is not subject to polarity because it is also the unity of being and non-being. This is consistent with Tillich's fundamental ontology: that in God, distinction is balanced by unity, whereas in humanity, it is not. To say that God is 'living' is to 'assert that he is the eternal process in which separation [i.e. actualization] is posited and overcome by reunion'.[48]

For Tillich, Creation is an expression of God's freedom; so creation is not 'contingent', according to Tillich, 'it doesn't "happen" to God, for it is identical with his life.'[49] This raises an important distinction between God, and God's 'life': God as 'living', like all of Tillich's descriptions of God, must be symbolic; awareness of the process of actualization, of the divine life, cannot exhaust God. Being a creature is to be rooted in the creative ground of the divine life and to actualize one's self through freedom.[50] However, because of the conflicts of existence, the imbalance of being and non-being, the freedom of creation, or humanity, is disrupted in an immediately, non-transcendent way for Tillich.

The concept of a living God has two intended consequences. First, existence includes a structural independence, a finite freedom given by God. Second, as the process of actualization, life remains connected to its creative ground. Human freedom is consistent with both the created structures of existence and with God's intention for creation.[51] Even in its distinction from the ground of being, human existence does not run the risk of being alienated from that ground. The structure and meaning of human life remains consistent with the life of God. For Tillich, 'What is valid for the individual is valid for history as a whole.'[52] The discussion of infinity and finitude is Tillich's answer to any rationalism that would deny the continued presence and activity of God in the world and the meaningfulness of human participation in that activity.

The persons of the Trinity are, at this point in the system, only evident in principle. Tillich does, however, forecast these principles in his discussion of the living God as 'moments within the process of the divine life'. The first principle is the Godhead, the transcendent 'ground of being'; the second principle is the *logos*, which opens the divine ground and brings meaning and structure; and the third principle is the 'actualization of the other two', the Spirit, in which all is contained and united. Through these principles, 'the finite is posited as finite within the process of the divine life, but it is reunited with the infinite in the same process'.[53] God can only be truly infinite if he has the finite posited within him, and if it is united with his infinity. Otherwise, finitude would stand in opposition to infinity, and thereby place limitations on it.

PROBLEMS WITH TILLICH'S DOCTRINE OF GOD

In equating the living God with 'being-itself', Tillich is trying to avoid calling God 'a being'. However, 'God is being-itself' is the single greatest source of critique of his theology, and elicits more or less sympathetic responses. Some find it helpful to distinguish the different senses in which Tillich's theological approach is 'ontological'. As rational inquiry, ontology can provide an approach to the discussion of God. As the response to the psychological shock, or threat, of non-being, however, ontology is an inquiry into the essential origin of existential experience.[54] These two meanings can also be related to two basic categories borrowed from Heidegger: ontology as 'existentialist' and as 'traditional'.[55] Traditional ontology is identified with structural and theoretical models of the relationship of infinite and finite being, which seek to establish what exists and what is known. Existentialist ontology is concerned with the human pursuit of meaning, the articulation of the question about the meaning of being, the doctrine of man. The existentialist approach to ontology is about human experience, as opposed to the logic of establishing the existence of anything.

While the distinction is helpful, it should not be mistaken as indicating a preference for the rationalistic or for the psychological, nor should it be used to characterize Tillich's project as psychological. For Tillich, the so-called traditional and existential approaches to ontology are inseparable; all ontology is a theological task. He calls for the correlation of existential questions about structure, and theological answers about meaning, within a system in which theology sets the entire agenda. Ultimately, ontology is human-concerned, but divine-centred.

Nonetheless, there is a strong critique of the universality of human experience in Tillich's ontological system, and its basis as a description of the universality of revelation. For some, Tillich assumes the identity of those driven to ask the ontological question and those who engage in the religious quest.[56] This involves two steps: first, the human question of being is described as universal, and anxiety over non-being is made into a doctrine of man; and second, the universal question is illuminated by religious symbols. This leads to a critique of two statements Tillich makes that seem to permit an alarming human awareness of God. First, that 'The question of God is possible because of an awareness of God present in the question of God';[57] and second, that humanity has an 'ontological awareness of the Unconditional'.[58] This implies that the doctrine of man itself embodies an answer to the ontological question. An ontological knowledge of God as being-itself, however, would seem to open Tillich to the charge of natural theology.[59]

To clarify, Tillich's use of the term 'awareness' is never actually clear, however, the two statements quoted above should be disambiguated. In the *Theology of Culture*, 'ontological awareness of the Unconditional' suggests that, by virtue of being finite, humanity can infer the possibility of that which is infinite. This gives no indication that humanity's intuitive 'awareness' of this Unconditioned is complete, self-conscious or exhaustive. In this case, awareness means logical inference, not intuition. In the *Systematic Theology*, the logical capacity of the human subject to formulate questions about God is dependent on the assumption that this is a God-given capacity. 'Man is the question he asks about himself', but humanity is not the source of the answer. Tillich also assumes that 'If God were not also in man so that man could ask for God, God's speaking to man could not be perceived by man'.[60] In this case, awareness of God refers to the fact that God created humanity, which includes its capacity to wonder, not that humanity is immediately and comprehensively aware of God. For Tillich, the human capacity to ask the question of God indicates the real capacity to begin to understand the revealed answer, not to formulate or discover it apart from revelation.

A second critique of Tillich's concept of God concerns the conflicting results yielded by the statement that God is being-itself, and the statement, in *The Courage to Be*, that there is a 'God above God'.[61] The apparently radical nature of the phrase 'God above God' is the subject of many commentaries linking it to many things, including a Böhmian *Ungrund*,[62] a desire to assert Christianity as the highest religion,[63] and even of being possible evidence in support of interpreting Tillich's Godhead as a quaternity.[64] Such readings, however, read Tillich's 'God above God' out of context, and expose the necessity of suspicion where Tillich's use of concepts and terminology is concerned.

The assumption that the concept of the 'God above God' stands within the long tradition of Christian mysticism is erroneous. This causes great difficulty for Tillich's interpreters, especially in relation to his ontology. On the one hand, the concept of 'being-itself' is problematic because it is 'beyond essence and existence', but is also 'said to have the character of becoming or process'.[65] On the other hand, the 'God above God' sounds overly remote and ineffable. 'One is the super-transcendent deity, beyond any predication whatsoever, the other the involved God whose life is strictly analogous to earthly life processes and which in Jesus Christ became identical with them.'[66]

Of course, Tillich's intentions are apologetic: to transcend theisms which reduce God to an empty slogan, and which are overly personalistic, naturalistic or dualistic. Yet, some clarification is required. First, Tillich defines God as beyond essence and existence or, more accurately, as beyond the distinction between essence and existence.[67] However, 'God is not a being out there. It is an experienced reality . . . God is not a purely objective reality.'[68] God's 'beyond-ness' does not suggest that God occupies some realm separate from essence and existence, but that God transcends their competition or tension. Humanity experiences existence as distorted essence, but there is no distortion in God. The Creator holds together in perfect unity that which humanity experiences as conflicted. However, that God transcends distortion does not imply that God is removed from the human experience.

Second, the phrase 'God above God' requires more context. Despite its apparent similarity to a mystical God 'beyond' the personal God of the Christian Gospels, for Tillich, the 'God above God' is a highly specific and Christian concept. Tillich says that 'The concept of absolute faith is the "God above God". Absolute faith and its consequence, the courage that takes the radical doubt, the doubt about God, into itself, transcends the theistic idea of God.'[69] The discussion that follows this definition consistently employs not the abbreviated 'God above God', but the phrase, 'the God above God of theism'. This God transcends theism and objectification, not reality. The God above God is not a supranatural entity, but a God who is revealed in and experienced by human life and history.

According to Tillich, the primary deficiency of all theistic accounts is the same: they allow no account of the radical doubt that results from the threat of non-being, the anxiety of the human condition. The remote God of theism offers no account of how the universal becomes concrete, of how infinite meaning can be communicated to finite human existence. In the personal and transcendent God of Christianity, Tillich finds a God 'above the God of theism'; that is a concept of God that can account for both divine transcendence and divine immanence in a way that offers *telos* and meaning to human life and history. The 'God above God' is necessarily personal, not remote.

Moreover, in *The Courage To Be*, Tillich points to the symbols of Christian theology – the Cross and the Resurrection – as the mediators of courage because they take doubt and meaninglessness into themselves. In the *Systematic Theology*, the Cross expresses God's subjection to existence, and the Resurrection attests to the conquering of existence.[70] For Tillich, revelation is only final, that is, authoritative, when it overcomes its finite conditions by sacrificing, and thereby transcending, its finitude.[71] The Cross and the Resurrection are the symbols of final revelation, for Tillich. The *Systematic Theology* describes God as taking on estrangement and conquering it for humanity. God remains manifest in the process of essentialization, in the Spirit and through the Spiritual Community, and provides courage to anxious humanity.

In sum, the God of Being, of Existence, and of History, the living God, is the only God who can account for the anxiety of existence, yet remain transcendent. That is, only the living God, can be the 'God above the God of theism'. The God above God is not a remote deity, nor does it contradict the concept of God as 'the power of being-itself'. Placed back in its context, the God above God is not a super-transcendent concept, but is a concept of divinity that encompasses both infinite transcendence and finite participation: the personal, living God.

In the first volume of the *Systematic Theology*, Tillich is laying the groundwork for a Trinitarian concept of God that follows the pattern of essentialization. Although it is not conceptually rigorous, the description of infinity as a 'quality' aligns it with the concept of the 'power of being-itself'. In so doing, Tillich suggests that divine essence is not a polarized 'nature' and 'freedom', but that the nature of God is itself free. In this way, he can locate both the pattern of existence and the possibility of human existence to transcend existence, in divine essence. Infinity is an indication, early in the *Systematic Theology*, that the dialectic of essentialization is what guides the entire system. This is more clearly demonstrated in the subsequent sections of the system, especially in the second volume's consideration of revelation as the 'power of being-itself' in the Christ.

CHAPTER FOUR

EXISTENCE AND THE CHRIST

Having described the essential ground of human existence in the first volume of the *Systematic Theology*, the second volume describes the Christ as the revelation of 'undisrupted essence', which 'appears under the conditions of existence'. This volume of the system has two main sections. The first describes the radical nature of estrangement, or sin, and humanity's inability to overcome it autonomously. The second describes the universal significance of the event of Jesus the Christ for human existence. In his earlier works Christ is identified chiefly with the concept of *kairos*, as a foretaste of the Kingdom breaking into history in 'the fullness of time'. In the *Systematic Theology*, while the concept of New Being retains this sense, it also emphasizes the universality of Christ as the reconciliation of human estrangement. In describing Christ in terms of 'being', as undisrupted essence appearing under the conditions of existence, Tillich relates the universal condition of estrangement and the desire for transcendence to the Christ event.

SIN, ESTRANGEMENT AND THE NEW BEING

In the first volume of the *Systematic Theology*, Tillich focuses the task of theology on describing the connection between 'message' and 'situation'. He describes this connection ontologically: the revealed God, as the perfectly balanced poles of being and non-being, or infinite 'being-itself'; and finite humanity, the imbalanced forces of being and non-being constitutive of 'human being'. This ontological description of revelation and the human condition allows Tillich to argue that the two are inherently related. This makes the significance of revelation for humanity not a matter of choice or intellectual decision, but a necessary condition of existence. However, this ontology does not describe the radical existential problem of estrangement, which is the impetus for Tillich's entire systematic endeavour of relating the significance of the Christian symbols. Where the ontology of the first volume of the *Systematic Theology* describes the conditions required for revelation to have meaning for humanity, the second and third volumes describe how human existence is *transformed* by the revelation of essential human nature in Christ, and what happens to existence as a result.

Tillich uses the dynamic dialectic of essence, existence and essentialization. The typology of being, non-being and being-itself can only express, for Tillich, the first two 'levels' of ontological analysis: the elements that constitute the ontological structure; and the ontological question itself. The third level of ontological analysis, however, 'expresses the power of being to exist and the difference between essential and existential being', while the fourth level considers these in light of the 'categories of existence': time, space, causality and substance.[1] The ontology of being and non-being, primarily in the first volume of the *Systematic Theology*, describes the forces of being and non-being as constitutive of both essence (being-itself) and existence (humanity), in order to demonstrate that they are related. The rest of the system, however, is devoted to describing what that relationship looks like within time and space, and what this implies about human freedom and the meaning of human history.

The finitude, or faultiness, of humanity as it *exists* implies, for Tillich, the idea of 'essential' humanity – humanity without or, in a mythological sense, before the conditions of existence. The biblical expression of 'essential' humanity is in the Garden of Eden. Eden, for Tillich, is the state of 'dreaming innocence', a description of ideal humanity which, though created and therefore differentiated from God, exists without knowledge of or anxiety from the perturbations normally associated with real human existence.[2]

Existence is characterized, in theological terms, by 'sin', whose origin is said to be in 'the Fall'. For Tillich, the biblical account of the Fall is a symbol of estrangement from God; 'The Fall is not a break [from ideality], but an imperfect fulfilment'.[3] The Fall is not merely a symbol of the movement from ideality to reality, as it is for many moments in Western philosophy; the Fall cannot be fully demythologized, says Tillich, but only 'half-way demythologized'. He notes, for example, that even when Plato replaces specific, mythological terms with the abstract terms of 'essence' and 'existence', he still uses the metaphor of 'the fall of the soul'.[4] The state of perfection prior to the Fall suggested in Genesis refers not to perfect existence, but to an analogical 'dreaming innocence' which is logically prior to the decision for self-actualization.[5] Tillich suggests, 'dreaming innocence' for two reasons: first, to ensure that only God is perfect; and, second, to account for a state in which humanity is finitely free, but prior to the decision to become self-actualized, which Tillich also calls 'temptation'.

The marks of human estrangement resulting from the Fall are collectively called 'sin'. In the individual the marks of sin are manifest as unbelief, hubris and concupiscence.[6] Unbelief, says Tillich, is not denial of God as such, since he who asks for God is already estranged from God. Rather, unbelief is the conscious separation of human will from God's will. Hubris is the result of the self-elevation of humanity to the realm of infinity, by the identification of partial truth as ultimate truth. Concupiscence is the unlimited desire to draw the whole of reality into oneself; it is a never-satisfied desire for self-fulfilment, and results in self-destruction and self-negation.

Estrangement is described in terms of the ontological polarities of freedom and destiny, dynamics and form, and individualization and participation which disrupt existence. With the separation of freedom and destiny, humanity places the individual at the centre of the universe; freedom turns to objects, persons and things contingent upon the subject. The lack of relationship between subject and object makes existence arbitrary, not free; without union to the will of God, human will is compelled by mechanical necessity, not destiny, a condition which Tillich calls the 'bondage of the will'.[7] Separated from form, dynamics becomes chaos; separated from dynamics, form becomes law. The separation of the inclinations towards individualization and participation can lead both to 'depersonalization', the objectification of subjects, and to the abstraction of the cognitive subject to the point of its estrangement from the world.[8]

For Tillich, however, this implies that sin is not merely the result of turning away from a law or from God. Rather, sin is inherent in human existence. Tillich is not intentionally assigning the blame for sin to God's act of creation, but broadening its definition. He wants to challenge the notion of sin as a numeric tabulation of wrong deeds according to a set of criteria. For Tillich, individual responsibility for sinful behaviour is the result of the much more fundamental human condition of estrangement from God. Thus, he defines estrangement as both fact (*Tatsache*) and act (*Tathandlung*):

> Sin is a universal fact before it becomes an individual act, or more precisely, sin as an individual act actualizes the universal fact of estrangement. As an individual act, sin is a matter of freedom, responsibility, and personal guilt. But this freedom is imbedded in the universal destiny of estrangement in such a way that in every free act the destiny of estrangement is involved and, vice versa, that the destiny of estrangement is actualized by all free acts.[9]

The doctrine of the universality of estrangement is not meant to be deterministic, nor is it meant to 'make [the human] consciousness of guilt unreal'.[10] It is meant to 'liberate' the individual from the unreal expectation of choice, of undetermined and unlimited freedom, for good or bad, for God or against God.

These stages of humanity are not historical, but are descriptions of every human life which is caught within the necessity and anxiety of self-actualization. 'The Fall' describes a necessary condition of human life, for Tillich: estrangement, or the self-awareness of finitude. No human ingenuity or intellect can overcome existential finitude because every human thought and action is equally limited by the conditions of existence. Salvation is sought through religion, legalism, asceticism, mysticism and sacramentalism,[11] but humanity is incapable of salvation because all of these efforts only elevate or repress what is finite. This limitation is the 'bondage of the will': the inability to break through estrangement. Existence which is estranged and only finitely free cannot, by its own efforts, reconcile itself to or reunite itself with its essential or true nature. The desire for reunion with its essential nature drives humanity to sin and to elevate that which is finite, especially itself. Incapable of rectifying its estrangement, and driving itself ever closer to self-negation and self-destruction, humanity can only be saved by the revelation of its essence in an undisrupted way.

In the first volume of the *Systematic Theology*, Tillich had described the finitude of the human situation. The dialectical polarity of being and non-being was balanced in essence, but unbalanced in existence. This helped describe the human condition in two ways: as conflicted and incapable of transcending its own finitude; and as desirous of resolution or the transcendence of this condition. For Tillich, the 'question' of human existence implies a 'quest' for revelation. The human quest is a longing for something new, for what is unambiguous, or beyond conflict and bondage, which replaces its own finite and ultimately failed attempts at transcendence. The answer, as we have seen, is the revelation of being-itself, the experience of being 'grasped' by the power of being-itself.

In the second volume of the *Systematic Theology*, the more general concept of 'revelation', or of human reason being 'grasped', is given definition in the historical event of the Christ. Tillich identifies the necessity for revelation in terms of the fallenness of human existence, and the need for revelation in terms of the need for an appearance of 'New Being', or 'essence' that 'appears under the conditions of existence'. If the sinfulness of humanity is both an 'original fact' and a condition of 'spatial and temporal existence', then the conflicts of existence represent the universal human condition. As in the case of human finitude, only the revelation of an alternative to the polarized conflicts of existence can offer the transcendence that finite human freedom seeks. In Tillich's system, the 'quest' for transcendence is answered in the offer of the Christ. This symbol offers the revelation of New Being, the power of reconciliation within conflicted existence.

The revelation of being-itself that is capable of answering the questions of existence must come from outside the realm of disrupted human 'being'. Only a 'New Being' can produce a new action.[12] Yet, in order to be meaningful for existence, the revelation of being-itself must occur within existence. Therefore, the revelation of being-itself capable of transforming existence and history must be paradoxical – it must be both 'unconditioned essence' and yet appear 'under the conditions of existence', the appearance of trans-historical (unconditioned) meaning within history. The appearance of essence within existence in this way provides human history with an experience of essential humanity upon which it can reflect, igniting the teleological drive of existence towards reunification with essence. In other words, the redemption of existence that the New Being accomplishes is only *in principle*. The Spirit, or what Tillich calls the 'Spiritual Presence', continues to guide humanity and history towards its *telos*: the reunification of disrupted essence (i.e. existence) with undisrupted essence.

This distinction between essence and existence is a common one in philosophy. Tillich associates it with the Platonic description of essence as 'the ideal', the Aristotelian description of essence and existence in terms of potentiality and actuality, and more modern philosophical systems, like Hegel's, in which existence is described as a development of essence, or Dewey's, in which the reverse is true.[13] In general, in describing 'essential' humanity in contradiction to 'existential' humanity the philosopher indicates what humanity should be, or genuinely is, like. Tillich has already described the difference between essential and existential humanity through the typology of being and non-being: essential humanity is undisrupted, existential humanity is disrupted. What is left for Tillich to describe is how revelation guides human life and history to become undisrupted once again, or, in Tillich's system, how disrupted existence is reunited with its original, undisrupted essence. This process is called 'essentialization', or 'salvation'.

This account of estrangement and sin is not without problems. The 'leap' from essence to existence that Tillich calls a condition of existence is inaccessible to thought; Tillich even calls it 'irrational'.[14] However, the irrationality of the Fall, or of sin and estrangement, is not the problem. The problem is that Tillich simultaneously defines the Fall as a 'transition from essence to existence', and as a condition of existence which has no spatial or temporal particularity.[15] We will see in the next section how Schelling's positive philosophy results in a similar problem. The effort to ground reason of itself, without relying on negation, caused Schelling to describe the transition from essence to existence as a necessary 'leap'. Tillich's conflation of creation and the Fall may be the result of a similar goal: to retain the positive status of existence, even as disrupted essence, or 'not-God'.

In making the Fall an ontological condition, however, Tillich has made creation and the Fall coincide, such that sin is interpreted in terms of fate rather than responsibility.[16] The proximity of creation and the Fall appears to be necessary for Tillich's concept of the reconciliation of estrangement in the New Being.[17] The ontological association of sin and existence is meant not only to emphasize the universality of the human condition, but it also places revelation firmly beyond the reaches of cognition. In the first volume of the *Systematic Theology*, as we have seen, Tillich describes revelation variously as 'grasping' the human situation, and as an event whose occurrence and necessity cannot be logically deduced. The universality of fallenness ensures that there is no possibility for humanity to transcend its finitude and estrangement by its own means.[18] Existence does not merely suggest what the barriers to self-understanding are; it *is* the fundamental problem which precedes all specific problems concerning humanity.

To this situation comes the message of the Christ. The combined history of existential humanity, the Christ event, and human life after the Christ but 'under the dimension of the Spirit' is, for Tillich, 'salvation history'.[19] The process of the history of salvation, which culminates in the 'reunion' of essence and existence, Tillich calls 'essentialization'.[20] As the appearance of essence under the conditions of existence, the New Being provides the means of reunification for existence and essence. Christ incarnate is, according to Tillich, the appearance of essential humanity under the conditions of existence, which remains unconquered by those conditions. The New Being is both transcendent, divine essence and immanent, human existence. The Christ lives under and shares in the conditions of existence, suffers as a result, and finally conquers the polarity of existence. The New Being thus reveals true human nature and transforms history, past and future, redeeming the estranging polarity of being and non-being that otherwise dominates human existence. The event of the New Being, however, is only the beginning of the process of salvation – a process in which human life and history, that is existence, move closer, through experience and reflection, to reunion with original essence. In the concrete revelation of New Being the direction of history is revealed, as is God's intention for the salvation of humanity. For Tillich, in the New Being history is transformed into the 'history of salvation'.[21]

ADDRESSING THE PROBLEM OF HISTORICAL REVELATION

As infinity was a response to the problem of ontological proofs for God's existence, the discussion of Christology in the system arises out of the challenge of historical criticism. Tillich addresses the erosion of a secure, historical picture of Jesus of Nazareth in the late nineteenth and early twentieth centuries, and the consequent insecurity in the theological picture of Jesus 'as the Christ.' In the second volume of the *Systematic Theology*, Tillich makes changes to his earlier theology of Christ as *Kairos*. He redefines the Christ as the 'New Being', in terms of divine essence under the conditions of existence, and more closely aligns salvation with the ontological doctrine of the first volume. In the process, he interprets the significance of the

Christ as more than a collection of historical data, with a view to answering the challenge of the historical Jesus project.

The possibility of the 'new' first appears substantially in *The Interpretation of History* as the concept of Jesus the Christ as *kairos*. Tillich first describes *kairos* in opposition to the Utopianism popular in some of the religious socialist movements of the 1920s. Utopianism sees time fulfilled at some future point determined by human actions. In contrast, *kairos* suggests all that is distinctive in the Christian conception of time, namely, 'that time may be invaded by eternity, that it has a direction, that it has a centre . . . and that in time itself man may never achieve the fullness of the eternal'.[22] From the Greek for 'season', 'appropriate time' or 'time fulfilled', *kairos* is used instead of the other Greek word for time, *chronos*, which is commonly used to express time as a measurement.[23] This distinction is key: while *chronos* is quantitative, *kairos* is qualitative. It is a description of God's fulfilment of salvation at a time of God's choosing, and is meant to replace the false hope of utopian, human self-fulfilment. Because it is free to appear, the *kairos* is also 'grace' – that which 'holds the ultimate tension of being and non-being in creative harmony'.[24]

In this earlier work, and in the *Systematic Theology*, Tillich also describes *kairos* as the freedom of being-itself to make a leap into history, to transgress the realm of pure being. The Christ event is the central *kairos*, but Tillich suggests that there are 'kairotic' moments, or *kairoi*, throughout history. *Kairoi* occur when the realization of the *logos*, God's Word, or the eternal meaning of being, occurs; though they receive their meaning from the central *kairos*. This self-transcending capacity gives the concrete events of history eternal meaning. Without ceasing to be the stuff of this world, history can provide 'a vista on the eternal'.[25] Interpreted through the symbols of Christ and Kingdom, the meaning of history is 'found in the process whereby the divine, through the instrument of human freedom, overcomes estrangement through love'.[26] As we will see, the *kairotic* meaningfulness of history is central to Tillich's understanding of the direction of salvation history, or, the process of 'essentialization'. Glimpses of eternal meaning, freely present in the world, point humanity to the *telos* of history: reconciliation with essential human nature, represented in the symbols of the Kingdom of God and Eternal Life.

Tillich has been criticized for 'grafting' the notion of *kairos* onto Christ, for not doing enough to show why Christ is the *kairos*.[27]

Where the early Tillich is concerned, this is correct. Christology, Tillich says in earlier writings, describes 'the point at which something absolute appears in history and provides it with meaning and purpose'.[28] Yet, it is also the point at which 'a given *kairos* [is identified] with the universal logos'.[29] Christology is not a *proof* that Christ is the centre of history; it is only a 'possible answer to the basic question implied in history, an answer which can never be proved by arguments, but is a matter of decision and fate'.[30] By such a reading, Christ is the *kairos* because of fate, or the circumstances of history, and faith. 'The centre of history is acknowledged as a centre in an attitude in which there is decision as well as fate, grasping, as well as being grasped by it.'[31] That Christ is the centre of history is not an assertion made through documentation; a decision is required. Christology is a 'possible answer to the basic question implied in history, an answer, of course, which can never be proved by arguments, but is a matter of decision and fate'.[32] Christ is the *kairos* because of faith.

However, faith in Christ as *the* meaning-giving event of history is not simply the result of a faithful affirmation of this event over a host of other, equally impressive historical events. The Christ is the *kairos* of more than the supposed unity of eternity and humanity within the human realm. The true meaning of Christ as the *kairos* of history is in his self-negation. In living communication with being-itself, 'Jesus of Nazareth is sacrificed to Jesus the Christ'.[33] As the Christ, Jesus becomes transparent to the mystery of being-itself. 'Final' revelation, for Tillich, or revelation upon which all else is conditioned, occurs here, in the self-negation of the revealed Christ; a revelatory event in which 'only the eternal shines through'.[34] This is the absolute paradox of Christian theology. Humans are not capable of this act. Only being-itself is capable of sacrificing its own finitude in such a way that the infinite is revealed. It is in the reality and symbols of the Cross and the Resurrection, says Tillich, that Christ expresses universal significance.

Eventually, a change in terminology signals a change in emphasis where the Christ is concerned. In the *Systematic Theology*, Tillich describes Christ as the New Being. The sense of Christ as the event (*kairos*), which gives all other past and future historical events (*kairoi*) their meaning, is retained in the terminology of revelation as 'final', or self-negating and transparent to the mystery of being-itself, and 'dependent', or received in subsequent times and places.[35] However, in defining the Christ in terms of New Being, final revelation is also seen as a foretaste of the Kingdom of God. The Kingdom is not merely an instance of *kairos*, but the goal or *telos* of historical fulfilment, as well as the constituting element of the Spiritual Community, which is directed towards fulfilment of the Kingdom. In fact, in the *Systematic Theology* references to *kairos* and *kairoi* only occur in reference to the Kingdom of God and are absent from the second volume on Christ. This does not mean that Tillich has changed his mind, that Christ is no longer the *kairos* of reality, history and faith. Rather, the function of Christology in the system is slightly different than in previous writings, as the Christ is identified less as the *kairos* of history and more as the New Being. This reflects two concerns Tillich has at the time of the *Systematic Theology*: that the hopeful anticipation embedded in the concept of *kairos* expressed by the social Christian movement of post-First World War Europe is mitigated against by the horror of the Second World War;[36] and, that the notion of *kairos* is too close to a notion of history, and the assertion of historical accuracy, which allows the universal significance of the Christ event to wax and wane with historical findings.

In the *Systematic Theology*, 'Christology is a function of soteriology'.[37] The concept of Christ 'bring[ing] the New Being' defines the historical uniqueness *and* eternal significance of the Christ. The move away from Christ as *kairos* to Christ as New Being is likely a move away from a strongly historical theology towards a more ontological theology. This is echoed in Tillich's characterization of the 'task of present theology' as finding a new way to express the Christological substance, which, as we discuss in the next chapter, also leads to a reconsideration of Trinitarian thinking in the third volume of the *Systematic Theology*.

For now, Christ as the New Being shows Tillich's concern to describe the truth of Christ in a way not tied to the data of history. This reflects his concern to preserve the Christ of faith in the face of increasing challenges to the Jesus of history. The question remaining for Tillich is how a historically and existentially conditioned event can be evidence of an eternal divine–human relationship and the basis of universal salvation. This concern is expressed in Tillich's discussion of the insufficiency of the Christological 'two natures' doctrine.

In the previous section, we saw that Tillich's definition of infinity was meant to provide an alternative account of the connection between God and humanity. The concept of infinity as the 'call' of the 'power of being-itself' to human being, simultaneously describes human estrangement from God and God's will to actively seek reunion with estranged existence. Similarly, Tillich restates the doctrine of the two natures of Christ as a new expression of being-itself. As the New Being, Jesus the Christ is a unique statement of the power of being-itself under the conditions of existence – the appearance of perfect human essence within existence. As such, the significance of the New Being is not merely historical, or a matter of preference or faith, but is a universally significant, ontological event.

Christ described as 'two natures' is too historically conditioned for Tillich. In place of the 'two natures', Tillich suggests the concept of 'eternal God-man-unity', or 'Eternal God-Manhood' – what Tillich calls a 'dynamic-relational concept'.[38] The effect is to give priority to the universal significance of the event of the Christ, over the particular details of the event. 'In [Christ's] being, the New Being is real, and the New Being is the re-established unity between God and man.'[39] The New Being, the concept of existential essence, of *eternal* God-man-unity', changes the emphasis of Christology from historical necessity, to the underlying connection between God (being-itself) and the existent human being.

The greatest value of the shift in emphasis, from Christ as historical *kairos* to universal New Being, is the demonstration of the place of Christology within a larger theological account. New Being is not only the revelation of essence within existence; it is also being-itself manifest 'in the power of Spirit'.[40] The New Being is essence that lifts existence out of polarity, and is therefore the catalyst of essentialization. Jesus the Christ is still a figure of religious history, but is primarily, for Tillich, a new expression of human existence. This gives the Christ, the 'eternal God-man-unity', the advantage of emphasizing the universality of the Christ event, over and against its personal and historical character. Tillich is concerned that theology and faith not stand or fall on the Scriptural accuracies of geography or biography.[41] Certainly one answer to the criticisms of the historical Jesus is to conceptualize and give priority to the content of Scripture: 'The foundation of Christian belief is not the historical Jesus but the Biblical picture of Christ',[42] what in the *Systematic Theology* Tillich calls the *analogia imaginis*.[43] Once the Christ has occurred, it is possible to conceptually demonstrate the necessity of such an event within a framework of faith. Some consider this to be a strength of Tillich's theology that the New Being can avoid the charge of inconsistency between a historical Jesus and a symbolic Christ.[44] However, there are many problems with Tillich's account of the New Being and its apparent independence from the historical Jesus.

Interestingly, Tillich's response to historical criticism also includes high praise for its ability to help clarify the meaning of Christian symbols by distinguishing their historical, legendary and mythical character. The theological symbol develops in four steps, for Tillich: it arises out of religious culture and language; it answers existential questions; it is used to interpret a historical event; and it becomes distorted by popular superstition.[45] Historical criticism, however, enables the theologian to point out some of the common errors of literalism and supranaturalism and disentangle the symbol from some of its distortions. As an example, Tillich traces the development of the symbol of 'the messiah' through its four stages: first, in Hebrew scripture and literature the messiah is the figure through whom God will establish his kingdom and justice; second, the present age is interpreted through an understanding of the messianic age to come; third, Jesus is received as the Christ, the messiah; and finally, the symbol is distorted by a literalism which sees the messiah as a human figure with supernatural powers. Tillich argues that, through these historical steps, the messiah loses its paradoxical meaning and the symbol is distorted. Historical criticism, however, makes it possible to recover this and other symbols from the distortions of literalism and supranaturalism by drawing attention to the different ways in which the symbol is used throughout history.

PROBLEMS WITH TILLICH'S DOCTRINE OF THE NEW BEING

First, the over-conceptualization of the Christ event is problematic, for at least three reasons. In wanting to interpret the biblical picture symbolically, Tillich bypasses the very details that permit the biblical narrative to be an account of the Christ as the New Being.[46] Furthermore, the symbol of the New Being conceptualizes the very thing Scripture insists must not be conceptual, God's personal encounter with humanity, and puts into question all manner of Scriptural detail. If Jesus of Nazareth is not necessary to the manifestation of New Being, then all biblical personalities, prophets, kings, judges, are also only incidental. It is not clear how the 'biblical picture', what Tillich calls the *analogia imaginis*, can produce the New Being while Jesus of Nazareth cannot. Even more troubling for Tillich is the possibility that if temporal and historical specificity are only incidental then the very concept of *kairos* as an appropriate time of God's manifestation is not just diminished, but demolished.

Second, the concept of the New Being makes too neat a distinction between the biblical picture of the Christ and the historical Jesus. The difference between faith and historical truth cannot be absolute, as both require the interpretative involvement of a judging subject. Similarly, the truth of faith must, at least to some degree, be based on historical truth, otherwise it is not an *analogia imaginis*, but simply *imaginis*. Matters of faith transcend the jurisdiction of historical truth even if they arise out of it.[47] Tillich is concerned that the universal significance of the Christ not be diminished by the increasing criticism of historical research. However, to some extent both the concept of the biblical picture of Jesus the Christ and the New Being depend on historical fact.

Third, abandoning the particularity of Jesus in favour of the universality of Christ may indicate a troubling departure from the Gospel. The *analogia imaginis* is not strong enough to count as an assertion of truth. Some argue that Christ as 'biblical picture', as distinct from historical fact, is a plain insertion within Tillich's system that does not assert anything more than a myth.[48] Finally, Tillich's ontological New Being does not even seem to require the scriptural Jesus Christ.

The concept of the New Being cannot replace the theological affirmation of the historical and personal Christ. While the attempt fails, Tillich's intention is to fit the Gospel message within his apologetic and existential method, and the *analogia imaginis* is the result of faith requiring more than historical detail. Tillich's 'theontological language' does not prove the historical fact of Jesus, but it does, 'demonstrate that the appearance of the New Being, in an historical and personal form subject to the conditions of existence, is the only form in which the answer to the question of existence could be given, *should that answer be possible*'.[49] However, Tillich's biblical picture is ultimately too formless, and the ontological category of the New Being lacks the specificity that the bearer of New Being requires in order to be New *Being*.

In sum, the movement from *kairos* to New Being demonstrates Tillich's concern that the Christ event not be circumscribed by historical findings, and that the content of revelation itself not be determined by the structure of the existence which seeks it. The description of the

Christ event in ontological terms is meant to avoid theology becoming heteronomous imposition. However, Tillich makes too many compromises in order to preserve his apologetic approach. A theological method may need to account for the advance of historical research, but Tillich's concept gives too much of the uniqueness of Christ away, even in its attempt to preserve Christian uniqueness. Nonetheless, the whole of the system must be borne in mind. The New Being is a statement of divine essence 'under the conditions of existence' and is the fundamental revelatory expression of essence, perfectly balanced being and non-being, to humanity.

Yet, the New Being is not the end of God's revelation. While it casts light on them, the New Being is neither the *terminus* of existential ambiguity nor the *telos* of human life. The salvation accomplished in the Christ event changes the meaning of human history, but is not the end of it. Humanity is guided towards its *telos*, expressed in the Kingdom of God and Eternal Life, by the Spiritual Presence. In fact, Tillich relies more on the doctrine of Spirit than on the doctrine of Christ to describe the reconciliation between the divine life and human life.

CHAPTER FIVE

THE SPIRITUAL PRESENCE AND TRINITARIAN THINKING

With the event of the New Being as the Christ, polarity is redeemed, and the possibility of transcendence through salvation becomes a real possibility in history itself. In the paradoxical grace of the revealed Christ, the meaning and goal, or *telos*, of history is revealed: the reunion of existence with its essence. However, 'essentialization', the reunifying activity of salvation history, is a continual process that occurs under the guidance of the Spiritual Presence.

LIFE AND HISTORY

'Life' is the term Tillich gives to the continued actualization of potential, and the mixture of existence and essence in the movement towards essentialization.[1] As a mixture, life is ambiguous. The change of terminology, from 'disrupted essence' to 'ambiguous' life, indicates not only the Christ's power to reveal an alternative to disruption and polar conflict, but also the continuation of the history of salvation and process of essentialization. The ongoing history of salvation is a 'spiritual process' and, for Tillich, human life occurs 'under the dimension of the Spirit'. The human spirit is a 'dimension' of the divine life, where dimension is a metaphor to describe the finite spirit as an element of the divine life in a way that suggests a connection, but which does not suggest that by its relationship it can compel the divine life. Spirit implies concepts like 'soul', 'mind' and 'reason', which in isolation distort the essence of being human, but which together have the effect of distinguishing humanity from other organic life.[2]

In *The Courage To Be*, Tillich describes human activity under three categories: participation, individualization and transcendence, that is, the courage to be part of a larger whole, to be independent and to accept these two conditions as the result of life lived within the encounter of human being with the power of being-itself. In the third volume of the *Systematic Theology*, these concepts are referred to as the three 'functions' of life: self-integration, self-creation and self-transcendence. For Tillich, 'life' is the actualization of potential which occurs 'under the dimension of Spirit'. This is meant to indicate that human life is both essential and existential; that humanity lives in the presence of God, but nonetheless experiences estrangement. As a result, each function contains its own dialectical movement within finite limitations, and each requires the Spiritual Presence of God to transcend those limits. This means that each function of life is, initially, characterized by ambiguity.

Self-integration encompasses knowledge of oneself, which Tillich calls self-identity; encounter with the other and a resulting self-alteration; and renewed knowledge of oneself called 'return to oneself'.[3] The movement of self-integration is reflective and, therefore, circular. The results of this movement, of 'going out' and 'return', are ambiguous because they involve risk. As the human individual encounters both his environment and world, he can cognitively oppose himself to every element, ask questions, and receive answers and commands – freedoms and responsibilities. In the process, he decides either to alter himself or remain the same, but each decision is a decision regarding self-integration.

A further response of the self-integrating individual to his own self-alteration is to alter that which is around him, to create new 'centres', which Tillich describes in terms of horizontal movement.[4] Individuals are creative and encounter one another through a universe of shared meaning, which occurs by the functions of language and technology. Yet, self-creativity through words and technology is also ambiguous. Words not only enable transcendence of environment, but also place distance between meaning from the reality to which they refer. Technology not only liberates, but also leads to the objectification of environment and persons. Though subject to ambiguity, the praxis of 'receiving each other' in community, including through cultural acts of art, bridges both epistemological and ethical gaps among individuals.

Self-transcendence is the function of life which does not embrace its limitation, but which seeks that which is beyond it, in a vertical movement.[5] Even self-transcendence, however, is ambiguous, because it is both the greatness and the tragedy of life: the great aspiration to that which is tragically unattainable. This is no more true anywhere than in religion, despite its claims to be the answer to ambiguities. Religion duplicates ambiguity as it inevitably succumbs to the influence and presence of the profane and the inclination towards the institutionalization of finitude. Holiness, expressed through ritual, doctrine and art, comes to be identified with these finite forms, which Tillich calls the demonization, or distortion, of the divine.

Yet, while religion is not itself the answer to the quest for unambiguous life, the answer can be received through religion. Religion, specifically the Christian religion, has 'produced', according to Tillich, the three main symbols of unambiguous life: the Spirit of God, which symbolizes the presence of the divine life within the creaturely life; the Kingdom of God, which symbolizes the struggle and *telos* of history; and Eternal Life, which symbolizes the transcendence of servitude to the categorical limits of finitude themselves.[6]

Like life, history is also ambiguous. It is objective in the sense that people and places exist, and that events occur involving them. However, reflection on the meaning of these events is always subjective, as it arises out of a specific context, consciousness and tradition. Tillich describes the ambiguity of history within the same categories by which he describes the ambiguity of life in general. The ambiguity of history is first expressed in self-integration, as the will-to-power.[7] Using the example of the United States and the Soviet Union, Tillich personifies the will-to-power in history as 'empire building,' the vocational consciousness of a historical group. This inclination is a destructive one, ultimately resulting not in power but in powerlessness – empires come and go. The self-affirmation of different history-bearing groups, as with different individuals, causes competition and conflict. Second, ambiguity arises out of human self-creativity.[8] This is expressed in revolution and reaction. Tillich uses the example of conflict as a result of generation gaps. In order to bring in 'the new', younger generations must make changes to or discard 'old modes and structures'. This kind of revolution may be 'unfair', notes Tait, but is a necessary by-product of the process of self-creativity.[9] Consequently, aware of their achievements and the greatness of the past, older generations react against change. Again, conflict is the result. Finally, ambiguity is present in the human inclination towards self-transcendence, the self-elevating claim to ultimacy.[10] This is particularly noticeable in conflicts between religious groups, all claiming to possess the ultimate truth, resulting in holy wars and persecution.

Each of these descriptions of ambiguity under the historical dimension assumes participation in society. This is because, for Tillich, the quest for the solution to ambiguous life under the dimension of history involves communal action in addition to individual reflection. The Kingdom of God is not *nirvana*; that is, the individual is neither trying to escape his individual or communal identity, nor the conditions of historical existence. Rather, the Kingdom is a symbol which represents the resolution of ambiguous historical existence *within* history, by demanding participation under the guidance of the Spiritual Presence. Thus, the meaning of history is revealed (though never fully comprehended) within history, even though its meaning is derived from beyond history, from its ultimate goal.

The Kingdom is also an expression which gives a positive valuation to history, in contradiction to various negative concepts of history. These include the non-teleological interpretation of history, which Tillich identifies with nihilism; the tragic, or Greek notion of history as inevitable 'cycle'; the mystical, neoplatonic concept which tends to devalue history; and the mechanistic, or reductionist, view of history. In each, the notion of participation is obviated by a different form of pessimism. However, Tillich is also critical of overly transcendent views of history, such as Hegel's progressivistic model of immanent transcendence,[11] and the other-worldly transcendence of the Kingdom, which he associates with Augustine. In these, history is transcended and its meaning is subsumed.[12]

Despite the insistence on participation, there is a tension common to the functions of self-integration, self-creativity and self-transcendence: the tension between the inclinations of 'self' and 'world'. Because of this tension, the functions of life, which also describe history, at first appear polar in their alternating experience of the posited subject and its environment.[13] In the first volume of the system, the inclinations of individualization and participation comprise a conflict of ontological elements within existence. Revelation is required to repair the deadlocked oppositions of disrupted existence. However, life 'under the dimension of the Spirit' is not deadlocked in this way. Each function of life describes not only a tension between self and world, but also a movement of self, under the dimension of the Spirit, away from tension towards resolution. Human existence, under the Spirit, is not inherently conflicted, but is capable of self-critique and self-understanding. For example, in self-integration, the opposition of an 'other' outside the individual results in the inclination to use the experience of encounter to alter oneself. The opposition of self and other, under the new rubric of dialectic, results in a starting point and two logically coherent, sequential steps: posited self and posited other, new understanding of self.

The non-polarity of the functions of life is also demonstrated in the fact that the dialectical movement of self-integration results in something new. Tillich qualifies what 'new' means. The 'new' individual who results from self-integration is not entirely new; only the New Being is entirely new. The altered self, like the creative community, still relies on the grounding creative force from which it receives its power and limitation. However, the dialectic of 'going out' and 'return' is capable of altering the original subject. The dialectical structure in operation here is not polar, but triadic, and depends on a concept of the continued revelation of the power of being-itself within history.

THE SPIRITUAL PRESENCE: POWER AND CRITIQUE OF THE SPIRITUAL COMMUNITY

The polarity of being and non-being that dominates the first volume is only a description of what human nature is without Christ and without the Spirit. The 'Spiritual Presence' is that manifestation of divine essence that 'elevates the human spirit into the transcendent union of unambiguous life and gives the immediate certainty of reunion with God'.[14] The Spiritual Presence is the presence of New Being by which the individual experiences surrender to and reunion with divine essence. Experienced corporately, the 'Spiritual Community' arises wherever and whenever New Being is present, as the estranging effect of autonomous self-elevation is repaired by the theonomous power of the Spiritual Presence. Finite expressions of community, including religion, are surrendered to the determination and direction of the Spiritual Community.[15] The Spirit of God fulfils self-transcendence, which is the aspiration of life, by maintaining the integrity of the individual and the community while liberating it from the contingencies of finitude.

In the third volume of the *Systematic Theology*, Tillich describes Spirit as the 'power of being-itself' and as the power of the New Being.[16] As divine essence, Spirit completes the Trinitarian description of God. As revealed Spiritual Presence, Spirit is the power that guides human life and history in salvation and essentialization. Like all statements about God, says Tillich, 'Spirit' is symbolic. The capitalization of the term distinguishes it as divine presence, as something different from the spiritual life of humanity in culture, morality and religion. The difference between the two is not meant to introduce a dualism between human and divine Spirit. Rather, for Tillich, metaphors that describe the relations of finite realms cannot apply to relationship between finite and infinite realms.[17] The problem, however, remains that human understanding is bound by finite language and symbols. Thus, Tillich prefers the terminology of 'dimension', by which divine Spirit and human spirit are thought of as mutually indwelling.

The phenomenology of the Spiritual Presence is drawn from the historical experiences of inspiration, of Word and sacrament, and of faith and love.[18] For Tillich, faith is 'the state of being grasped by the transcendent unity of unambiguous life', that is the Spirit. In this case, as in the case of all revelatory experience, 'being grasped' by the Spirit implies two assertions: the inability to verify this experience against some experimental criteria, and the experience as fulfilling reason not replacing or destroying it. Tillich does not want the experience of the Spirit to rely on appeals to emotion only, or to the rational only. The Spiritual Presence is experienced as reception and participation, that is, love.

The doctrine of the divine Spirit is consistent with Tillich's other definitions of revelation and of the other persons of the Trinity. Like revelation, the divine Spirit 'grasps' the human spirit; it cannot be compelled to indwell in the human situation by human spirit, as human spirit remains ambiguous, conflicted and disrupted, while divine Spirit is not. Like the Christ, or the New Being, the transcendence of the Spirit is expressed through its self-negation: 'the language which is bearer of the Spirit is universal because it transcends the particular encounter which it expresses in the direction of that which is universal, the *Logos*'.[19]

The divine Spirit does not, therefore, 'invade individuals', but groups.[20] The Christ is the presence of the divine Spirit without distortion; 'the Spirit who prepared Christ in Jesus is the same Spirit who prepares mankind for its encounter with New Being in him'.[21] The Spiritual Community fostered by the Spiritual Presence as communities are made 'new' in the 'existential experience' of the Christ. However, the Spiritual Community is not the Christian Church, neither is it found in any one Christian denomination, nor in the collection of

THE SPIRITUAL PRESENCE AND TRINITARIAN THINKING

all denominations. The Spiritual Community is the power and structure inherent in Christianity, the 'inner *telos*' of the religion. The
Spiritual Community arises wherever churches confess Christ as the
central manifestation of God's Kingdom in history.[22]

The distinction between the Church, or churches, and the Spiritual
Community is meant to keep the ambiguity of the Church separate
from the unambiguous Spiritual Presence of the power of being-
itself. The life of the Church is its struggle against the ambiguities of
existence, in the power of the Spirit. Under the Spirit the individual
experiences the New Being as creation and regeneration, as positive
paradox and justification, and as process and sanctification. In all of
its experiences, the Church attempts to actualize its essence, which is
the Spiritual Presence, but it is simultaneously judged by that essence.
Like the individual, the Church is prey to the self-elevating ambiguities of life. Tillich's 'Protestant principle' expresses the priority of the
Spiritual Presence over religion, its conquering of religion and its
victory over the profanization and demonization of the Church.[23]
This implies that the power of 'truth and love', are not the province
of the Church, but of the Spiritual Community it strives to be.

This description of the Spirit, or Spiritual Presence, supports
the argument concerning the significance of symbolic statements for
Tillich. Tillich's intention in restating the doctrine of the Spirit in
conceptual terms is not to empty it of specificity or to remove it from
particularity; the Spirit is intimately involved in human life and history. The purpose of Tillich's conceptual description of the Spirit,
and of God and Christ, is to ensure their independence beyond the
sum of historical experiences of them and to avoid an identification
of infinite and finite.[24] History and life, especially in the Church,
are ambiguous for Tillich; they are subject to distortion, hubris, self-
elevation, collectively called sin. Tillich's apologetic task is to differ-
entiate human ambiguity from divine unity, in order to make divine
unity the judge and salvation of human estrangement.

However, in the final section of the third volume of the *Systematic
Theology*, Tillich emphasizes the teleological nature of life and history 'under the dimension of the Spirit'. The universal meaningfulness
of the revealed Christ and the continued Spiritual Presence imply a
direction, or a *telos*, for life and history. This *telos* is no less than the
union of disrupted existence and divine essence, or essentialization,
the *telos* of salvation history, which is described in the symbols of the
Kingdom of God and Eternal Life.

THE KINGDOM OF GOD AND ETERNAL LIFE

The symbol of the revealed direction of history is the Kingdom of God. The Kingdom of God is a symbol of 'inner-historical' *telos*, a goal implicit in each act and moment of history. Yet, it is also the symbol of a 'trans-historical' *telos*: Eternal Life, which represents the meaning of all life and history, finally fulfilled and in complete unity with the divine.[25]

First, Tillich describes what he means by the 'inner-historical' Kingdom in four ways. In the Old Testament, the Kingdom symbolizes victory over the enemies of Israel. In later Judaism and in the New Testament, it is the transformed heaven and earth – a new reality, a new period. The political symbol is gradually understood as a cosmic symbol, without losing its political connotation. Tillich notes that Christ as 'King' retains a double connotation – a title both for saviour and 'victor'.[26] The Kingdom is also social, inspiring individuals and communities to seek holiness with the moral imperative of justice. It is not a utopia, because the justice it seeks is God's, not humanity's. 'Man actualizes himself as a person in the encounter with other persons within a community.'[27] The Kingdom is personal, as it heralds the *fulfilment* of humanity in every human individual, not an escape from human finitude or a denial of identity. Yet, the Kingdom is also universal, as it reveals the ultimate meaning and *telos* of all life.

According to Tillich, the promise of history is the eventual reunification of essence and existence, according to the process of essentialization. Insofar as this promise has been revealed in the New Being, in Christ, the goal of the Kingdom is revealed within history. 'There is no other event of which this could be asserted [though] the actual assertion is and remains a matter of daring faith.'[28] The intimate connection between Christ and Kingdom is not unique to the *Systematic Theology*. Elsewhere Tillich says that Christology 'periodizes' history into pre- and post-Epiphany periods. Before Christ's appearance, history is a period of preparation. After his appearance, there is no more preparation required, as *kairos*, the 'right moment', has arrived. 'In this moment, the reality of the Kingdom of God appears in a personal life and creates a new group with a new historical consciousness, the church. According to the feeling of this group, the end has arrived *in principle*.'[29]

The significance of this definition of *kairos* for the *Systematic Theology* is that the Christ, the embodiment of the Kingdom's *telos*, is not the temporal end of history; rather, life, time and history continue. However, in God's personal manifestation, the goal of history and the meaning of historical events are revealed. Christ is the central manifestation of God's promise; he is the *kairos* which gives previous and future *kairoi* their meaning. The Kingdom is understood as that enduring symbol of promise, of continuing participation of the eternal in the temporal realm, in the post-Epiphany period of history; or in the words of the *Systematic Theology*, of 'inner-historical' essentialization.

The structure of life, and now history, is dialectical insofar as it drives towards something new, something better. Thus, it is the *telos* of life and history that distinguishes the dialectic in the third volume of the *Systematic Theology* as essentialization, and not polarity. This is supported by Tillich's terminology; terms like 'drive', 'striving', 'direction' are used to describe the process of life, and history is described as 'running', or 'driving' towards the new.[30] For Tillich, any time life comes into conflict with itself and drives to a new stage beyond conflict, 'dialectics takes place'.[31] However, most central to a notion of history as teleological is Tillich's insistence that history happens *to* a meaning-bearing group, that is, to a community.

The Kingdom is the *telos* within all history, a symbol expressing the resolution of ambiguity. It submits the 'self-integrating' desire for control under the authority of the divine life and the principle of self-sacrifice. The ambiguities of 'self-creativity' in history appear within social growth, as the inclinations of revolution and tradition, while the ambiguities of 'self-transcendence' appear as the tension between the Kingdom of God as expected and as it appears.[32] Within history, the Kingdom is 'already' and 'not yet' – a symbol of historical change and of eschatological hope. The events of the Cross and the Resurrection and their impact on human existence are historical; but they also reveal and symbolize a meaning greater than their historical reality: the salvation, or essentialization, of all humanity.

Second, the symbol of Eternal Life is the 'trans-historical' symbol of essentialization. While the Kingdom symbolizes the unity of essence and existence experienced within human life and history, as a result of the *Kairos*, Eternal Life symbolizes the unity of human history and the divine life itself. The difference is simple. The 'inner-historical' symbol relates an ongoing process; ambiguities still require resolution, and this state of affairs is represented in the Kingdom as foretaste. The 'trans-historical' symbol, however, represents the end of the process, the state in which ambiguities are forever resolved; this is the Kingdom as arrived.

Embodied in the two symbols of the Kingdom and Eternal Life is the *telos* of history, however, not its *terminus*. The promise of life's fulfilment affects the past meaning of life and historical events, and present life and history. As L. Gordon Tait notes, 'The fulfilment of history does not happen on the last day of recorded time; it is always with us, breaking into our temporal order and elevating it to the eternal.'[33] In such a process, Tillich says that nothing which was created is lost, but what is positive about existence is disentangled from and elevated above what is negative. Nothing is lost because 'in the ground, the "aim" is present'.[34] Essentialization is not a return to an original, completely potential state. Rather, it is a process of return to and of 'adding something to'. Participation in the eternal life, says Tillich, 'depends on a creative synthesis of a being's essential nature and what it has made of it in its temporal existence'.[35]

Tillich's distinction between the inner- and trans-historical does not, however, represent a dichotomy. The distinction is only necessary in order to separate notions of the in-breaking Kingdom in history, which, as appearing within history, is fragmentary, and the vision of the Kingdom as it transcends these temporal 'victories'. This is also the link between human history and the history of salvation for Tillich. The two are not entirely identical, because human history remains fragmentary, while the history of salvation constitutes the moments in which the power of the Kingdom is asserted. Salvation history, then, cannot happen without world history because it happens within it; but salvation history is not bound by world history, but rather, fundamentally changes it. Likewise, the trans-historical is not supra-historical, in the sense that it is completely transcendent of time, space, or disconnected from human existence.[36] We should recall that, for Tillich, revelation is always revelation *to* humanity.

For Tillich, the human situation is conflicted and incapable of its own dialectical development; its goal of existential reunion with essence in Eternal Life, although an inherent part of its essence, is disrupted and obscured from view by sin, until Christ is revealed. That the source of existential *telos* is revealed in, but also transcendent of, history, ensures that revelation does not become reduced to mere events or people. The symbols of revelation, ultimately, always point beyond the finite, even as they require finite media to communicate with finite beings and minds. The positioning of two teleological symbols, the Kingdom within history and eternal Life outside of history, is meant to ensure both the ultimate transcendence and the universal meaningfulness of revelation.

SPIRIT-CHRISTOLOGY

There is very little written about Tillich's doctrine of the Spirit, or Spiritual Presence, owing mostly to the fact that Tillich's focus on the doctrine seems to be restricted to the last few years of his life. However, some suggest that in terms of the *Systematic Theology*, the concept of Spirit is the most central.[37] In the third volume of the *Systematic Theology*, Tillich identifies the divine Spirit as God and as the one who constitutes Jesus as the Christ and the power of New Being. The weight given to the doctrine of the Spirit in the third volume of the *Systematic Theology* has led one theologian to argue that Tillich's Christology is a 'Spirit-Christology' more than it is a 'Logos-Christology', something that could not be argued from the first two volumes of the *Systematic Theology*.[38]

The significance of this point cannot be underestimated. Most Tillich scholarship focuses on the first volume of the *Systematic Theology*. The bulk of the *Systematic Theology*, however, is focused on existence in terms of the Spirit and, therefore, human participation in the process of essentialization. Placing the Spirit at the centre of Tillich's system yields an entirely different perspective than if the doctrine of God as being-itself, or Christ as New Being, are taken as central. The divine Spirit, not being-itself or the New Being, becomes Tillich's central definition of divinity.

The basic ontology presented in the first volume of Tillich's system is that being and non-being are constitutive of essence and existence. This remains the case in the second and third volumes, but there is also a shift in focus in these volumes. According to the third volume, 'Christ is the presence of the divine Spirit without distortion'.[39] The focus moves from Christ as the point of embodiment or contact between undisrupted and disrupted essence, to the Spirit as that power which is embodied in Christ: the power of being-itself. Some have argued that the power of being-itself is only one ontological element in God, for Tillich, and that his notion of Trinity is not clear, as a result.[40] However, as that which is identified not only with the power of being and non-being, but also with the power of New Being and of the Spiritual Presence, the power of being is the concept that binds the triune God as a unity, for Tillich.

Seen in light of the dialectic of essentialization, the *Systematic Theology* equates the 'power of being' with the 'power of divine essence'. The identification of each member of the Trinity with the power of being-itself, or the 'power of being', provides the consistency among the creating activity of God as essence, of the relational activity of God under the conditions of existence, and of the salvific activity of God in the process of essentialization. Coupled with the third volume's emphasis on the activity of the Spiritual Presence as the power of divine essence re-established and operative within existence, Tillich's system is clearly focused on the power of being in the salvific task of the Spirit. The process of essentialization is still utterly dependent on the event of the Christ who as New Being unites essence and existence and, as the *Kairos*, redeems all history, past and present. But in Tillich's existential system, it is the divine Spirit, experienced by humanity as the Spiritual Presence, which guides all human activity and change according to the *telos* of God's Kingdom, and which facilitates the movement towards Eternal Life. That is, the divine Spirit is the power of being-itself to effect essentialization.

The life of the triune God is described according to the same concepts that describe human life. Both human life and divine life are, according to Tillich, essential, then existent, then essentialized, or reunified. The description of the divine Spirit as the power of being-itself is what makes the continuing events of human life and salvation part of the history and life of God. The human experience of essentialization is triadic because the divine life is triune, because humanity experiences its history and *telos* according to the pattern of God's revelation. This has caused one critic to read Tillich's doctrine of God as completely humanistic, or immanent.[41] Not only does this criticism ignore Tillich's distinction between the inner- and trans-historical symbols of essentialization, the Kingdom and Eternal Life, it also ignores Tillich's assertion that the persons of the Trinity are, ultimately, inaccessible symbols. If nothing else, the entire discussion of Spiritual Presence and the Spiritual Community achieves one thing: to distinguish between divine Spirit and human spirit. The Spiritual Community is not identified with any one church or group of churches. Tillich's concept of the Spiritual Community ensures that even though revelation occurs by finite means, allowing humanity to understand that revelation is *for* humanity, the truth it expresses is not finitely circumscribed.

The case of the Spiritual Presence underscores the crucial fact that, for Tillich, revelation occurs both in a way that is observable to human cognition and in a way that transforms and transcends cognition. That reason is 'grasped', and that the Spiritual Presence infuses and transforms human existence through participation in essence, does not suggest that 'God is humanity', but that humanity is revealed to and reconciled by a God simultaneously capable of transcendence and immanence. For Tillich, the critique of the Spiritual Presence is directed at the manifest and manifold churches, while the critique of the Protestant principle is directed at theology in general. Both concepts ensure that the hubris and self-elevation characteristic of human existence does not override the eternal meaning of its symbols. Always, for Tillich, the human condition is the evidence both of the need for revelation and of humanity's essential connection with and participation in the divine life.

TRINITARIAN THINKING: ADDRESSING DOCTRINAL DIFFICULTIES

Separate discussions of the doctrine of the Trinity in the *Systematic Theology* are brief. However, the centrality of the Trinity to Tillich's system cannot be contested. Not only is the *Systematic Theology* divided according to the persons of the Trinity, but God, whom Tillich describes as the 'power of being-itself', is also distinctly manifest in three persons, all of whom are integral to Tillich's concept of the history of salvation. The necessity of Trinitarian thinking arises, says Tillich, for three reasons. It arises first because of God's threefold manifestation as creative power, saving love and ecstatic transformation. Second, Trinitarian thinking is the result of tension between the absolute and the concrete elements of 'ultimate concern', which raises the danger of tritheism. Third, Trinitarian thought expresses the dialectical relationship between the human experience of revelation and the divine ground of being-itself.[42]

The importance of Trinitarian thinking, for Tillich, is in reclaiming what has become problematic. He thinks that the doctrine of the Trinity has been put 'on the altar' to be adored, revered as a mysterious riddle to be solved (*ST III*, 291). Ultimately, for Tillich, however, Trinitarian doctrine is different from 'the Trinity'. The Trinity is the 'eternal mystery of the ground of being' (*ST III*, 291), while Trinitarian doctrine is human thought about and reflection on the threefold experience of revelation. This distinction between object and concept is more than pedantic. If the persons of God will always remain mysterious and, to a large extent, inaccessible, then thought about them will be useful only insofar as it addresses the human situation and the meaningfulness of a triune revelation to humanity. Trinitarian thinking can be reopened and reclaimed as the human, symbolic description of the experience of revelation, and what it implies for the human situation.

It is helpful, then, to examine Tillich's discussion of the 'Trinitarian problem' as a separate, historical phenomenon, which involves his account of the rise of Trinitarian thinking in Christian theology and his insistence on the necessity of dialectical thinking. The doctrine of the Trinity appears explicitly only twice in the system, once in a discussion of the living God as 'actualized', and once in a discussion of the function of the Trinitarian symbols for the Christian religion.[43] Because of the relatively few words devoted to its explicit discussion, the significance of the doctrine of the Trinity in Tillich's theology has been critically underestimated.[44]

Tillich's most direct discussion of Trinitarian thinking occurs in the third volume of the *Systematic Theology*. As with other sections of the system, his concern in this discussion is to address particular problems in theology by reconsidering the doctrine. In the case of the Trinity, Tillich focuses on the historical difficulties arising from the confession of the two natures of Christ, and the need to 're-open' the discussion of the significance of Trinitarian thought. In the course of this brief discussion, however, Tillich definitively distinguishes between the paradox of grace and the dialectical nature of the Godhead. This distinction points to the Trinity as the primary symbol of dialectical theology.

The main problem in Trinitarian dogma, according to Tillich, is not unique to Christianity: 'it is impossible to develop a doctrine of the living God and of the creation without distinguishing the "ground" and the "form" of God, the principle of the abyss and the principle of the self-manifestation in God'.[45] The first difficulty, for

Tillich, in Trinitarian thinking is the basic conceptual problem of asserting both that God is transcendent and that God became manifest in human form. On the one hand, the Christological discussion begins when God's revelation is identified with the manifestation of the divine ground of being. Theological interpretation of the Christ event attempts to describe the universal impact of the particular historical event. On the other hand, the Trinitarian discussion begins with the practical reverence for this historical event. That is, liturgical devotion to the Christ raises a conceptual problem: 'The decision of Nicaea acknowledged that the Logos-Son, like the God-Father, is an expression of ultimate concern. But how can concern be expressed in two divine figures . . .?'[46]

The second difficulty is that the subsequent post-Nicaean confession of the divinity of the Spirit does not solve the basic conceptual problem. The resulting language of *personae* and *hypostasis*, according to Tillich, only provides a way of referring to the problem; it does not bring an end to the discussion. The final and compounding difficulty is that the centuries-old confession of 'one is three and three is one' was 'put on the altar, to be adored. The mystery ceased to be the eternal mystery of the ground of being; it became instead the riddle of an unsolved theological problem'.[47] Understood only as 'three is one and one is three', the doctrine of the Trinity is a distortion, 'a trick or simply nonsense'. Although it is not entirely clear for what kind or era of Christianity is the Trinity this kind of a riddle, it is clear that Tillich feels that the doctrine of the Trinity has become an esoteric doctrine. The solution to the Trinitarian problem begins by relating it to, and distinguishing it from, Christology.

Tillich's doctrine of the Trinity rests on two critical distinctions. The first is more implicit in Tillich's characterization of the history and logical necessity of the Christological confession for Trinitarian thinking: the Trinity is a concept used to make sense of issues raised by Christology. The second is more explicit: the Trinity is fundamentally dialectical. For Tillich, the doctrine of the Trinity can be recovered from problems, and made useful, if thought of as Christologically rooted and dialectical.

In the first volume of the *Systematic Theology* the Christological basis of the doctrine of the Trinity is asserted as a dogmatic necessity. 'Any discussion of the Christian doctrine of the Trinity must begin with the Christological assertion that Jesus is the Christ. The Christian doctrine of the Trinity is a corroboration of the Christological dogma.'[48] In the third volume, in addition to being a dogmatic necessity, the Christological basis of the Trinity is characterized more as logical necessity.[49] In his account of the Ecumenical Councils, Tillich suggests that, although the confession of the Trinity came before the distinction of the two natures and one person of Christ, Trinitarian thinking is the conceptual result of the issue of distinction and unity in God, which is primarily a Christological issue.

For Tillich, the Trinity is a helpful 'metaphysical' concept, that is, a way of talking about God as both diversity and unity.

[T]he Trinitarian doctrine is the work of theological thought which uses philosophical concepts and follows the general rules of theological rationality. There is no such thing as Trinitarian 'speculation' (where 'speculation' means conceptual phantasies). The substance of all Trinitarian thought is given in revelatory experiences, and the form has the same rationality that all theology, as a work of the Logos, must have.[50]

The doctrine provides a speculative description of the Godhead, a way of talking about God and the human experience of God that does not presume to be exhaustive of God.

Trinitarian thinking is further distinguished from Christology in that, while Tillich calls Christology 'paradoxical', he calls the Trinity 'dialectical'.[51] Previously, Tillich's distinction between paradox and dialectic referred to the difference between God's gracious self-manifestation and human knowledge of it. Here, the distinction is employed the same way. This is why Tillich argues that Trinitarian discussions actually begin with the Christological doctrine. The answer to the first problem implied in the doctrine of the Trinity, that God is transcendent and yet revealed, is the paradox of the Christ. The remaining problem in the doctrine of the Trinity is the problem of the diversity of revelation.

On its own, the paradox of grace gives no account of the human experience of revelation which, although not completely rational, is in some way available to cognition and reason. Yet, without a concept of paradox the distinction of persons within the Godhead becomes mere enumeration. Thus, the doctrine of the two natures of Christ is paradoxical. However, because of the importance of the Spiritual Presence, as the means by which humanity is both judged and saved, and as the power of being-itself and New Being, the doctrine of the Trinity is properly dialectical; that is, a symbol of the eternal and enduring process of divine self-manifestation, and of the continued human experience of that revelation.

For Tillich, Trinitarian confession remains possible, 'but it requires a radical revision of the Trinitarian doctrine and a new understanding of the Divine Life and the Spiritual Presence'.[52] True to his entire project, the effort to understand God by means of the Trinity is rooted in the human experience of revelation. The activity of the Christ is paradoxical, but the doctrine of Christ is the human expression of that paradox. In the same way, although expressive of dialectic, the Trinity is a symbol that helps humanity frame its experience of revelation and its continuing participation in the life and history of salvation.

The attention Tillich calls to the historical process of the early Church Councils, and to the necessity of the Christological doctrine as logically prior to the Trinitarian doctrine, can make Tillich's use of the Trinity seem merely pragmatic.[53] Because Tillich avoids the language of *ousia* and *hypostases*, some speculate that the distinction within the Trinity is, for Tillich, merely a result of the different existential questions arising out of the human predicament.[54] Tillich certainly does argue that the symbols of God, Christ and the Spirit answer the existential questions of finitude, estrangement and ambiguity. However, the unity of these symbols is not the result of an inability to distinguish the persons of the Trinity, but in each symbol's participation in the 'power of being-itself'. Their unity is in being-itself, which is God, and their diversity is in the unique manifestation that being-itself takes in the human experience of revelation. It is unclear from this, however, how Tillich's 'power of being-itself' and the 'symbols of revelation', as a description of the unity and diversity of the Trinity, is sufficiently different from the language of *ousia* and *hypostasis*. It may be, then, that the problem is more with Tillich's language of symbol than with his treatment of the Trinitarian discussion.

PART III

PHILOSOPHICAL THEOLOGY: CLARIFYING
THE CONCEPTUAL ROOTS OF TILLICH'S THEOLOGY

CHAPTER SIX

PHILOSOPHICAL CONCEPTS
AND STRUCTURES

Although it is clear that Tillich seeks to repair theology with the aid of existential analysis, it is also clear that there are some challenges associated with correlational theology. For example, Tillich has been criticized for simply imposing the concepts of *kairos* and New Being on the Christ, and for weakening Christological doctrine with the concept of the *analogia imaginis*. This raises questions about the strength of his systematic method at its most crucial point. We have also seen that Tillich employs two different dialectical approaches in the *Systematic Theology*. The first is the typology of being, non-being and being-itself; the second is the typology of essence, existence and essentialization. At first glance, these structures appear similar; however, they serve very different functions within the system. Here, we distinguish between these two internal structural patterns of the *Systematic Theology* by considering their philosophical origins. Clarifying the two different functions of dialectic helps us to see more clearly the mechanisms by which Tillich argues that revelation and the human condition are related.

   Of the major twentieth-century theologians, Tillich is the most committed to expressing revelation in terms of the human experience of it.[1] He clearly places himself in the Existentialist tradition of the nineteenth century, locating his approach to the human situation in a line that begins with Schelling and, albeit in ways of which Tillich is critical, a line that continues through Kierkegaard, Nietzsche and Marx. All of these philosophers of existence wrote largely in response to what they saw as the triumphalist essentialism of Hegel. In Hegel's account of 'Spirit' in the *Phenomenology* and 'the Concept' in the works on logic, they saw a description of historical dialectic which not only claimed to account for the diversity and self-consciousness of history and existence, but also placed each religion and culture of history within a progressive movement that culminated in the philosophical age of Hegel himself. They associated Hegel's approach with political hegemony, social oppression and the diminishment of human experience in favour of a speculative idealism.[2] Tillich seems to ally himself with the early existentialism of Schelling and Kierkegaard, as his references to Hegel tend to describe his philosophical system as inadequate, misleading, or at the very least, abandoned.[3]

Yet, Tillich does not slavishly adopt the positions of any philosopher. One of the frustrations of Tillich scholarship is uncovering, and keeping track of, all of the people from whom he borrows concepts to construct his theology. It would be misleading, therefore, to interpret Tillich as a 'Schellingian', despite his early concentration on Schelling. He is always most concerned that theology address the contemporary situation. To that end, philosophical concepts and systems are only as helpful as they are adaptable and able to 'answer' the existential questions of their time. However, a basic appreciation of the philosophical origin of some of his most central concepts will help Tillich's reader in two ways. First, it provides some of the background that he, after years of study, simply assumes. Second, it permits greater distinction between the original philosophical concept and Tillich's employment and adaptation of it.

Here, we briefly highlight some of the central concepts of the work of Schelling and Hegel in order to provide some clarity regarding Tillich's similarity to and significant distance from the conceptual and structural influences of his philosophical training. The consideration of Schelling occurs for obvious reasons. As we will see, the ontological structures of Tillich's system owe a great deal to Schelling. The dialectical pattern of the categories of life resembles Schelling's *Identitätsphilosophie*; his use of the forces of being and non-being as characteristic of essence and existence is also similar to Schelling's use of them. However, it is less clear, at least immediately, why Hegel should be considered as well.

The first indication for expanding the search for philosophical influences is that there are many concepts that Tillich introduces which have no easy parallel in Schelling. The self-negation of Jesus as the Christ; the Spiritual Presence as a critical as well as unifying, presence; the *telos* of history, the Kingdom, as both inside and outside of history; and the characterization of Eternal Life, the goal of essentialization, as both the reunion of existence with essence, and also the negation of what is negative in existence to create a new reality; these are not concepts derived from Schelling. The second indication that we have for finding a conceptual influence on Tillich outside of Schelling is that concepts such as the self-negation of Christ to reveal New Being, and the negation of what is negative in Eternal Life to produce a new state of being, bear at least some resemblance to Hegel's concept of an immanently transcendent dialectic and of Christianity as the consummate religion.

Of course, it would be just as misleading to interpret Tillich as 'Hegelian' as it would be to interpret him as a 'Schellingian'. Both philosophers frequently come up short in Tillich's estimation of systematic approaches to the perennial questions of existence. However, some scholarship on Tillich has noted the ways in which Hegel is conceptually, or at least structurally, present in Tillich.[4] As with Schelling, highlighting some of the major concepts of Hegel's dialectical approach will help both to understand some of the structural origin of Tillich's concepts and the ways in which he alters or departs from those concepts. In particular, the difference between Schelling's descriptions of dialectic and the Trinity and Hegel's are crucial for understanding Tillich's repositioning of traditional doctrine.

SCHELLING AND THE CONCEPTUAL STRUCTURE OF TILLICH'S ONTOLOGY

Ontology in Schelling

There is considerable debate, even still, over how to categorize and describe Schelling's philosophy. From his early association with Hegel in the late eighteenth century to his last lectures in the middle of the nineteenth century, the structure and focus of Schelling's systematic philosophical efforts changed considerably, and more than once.[5] However, it is generally possible to say that where Kant and Fichte separate the 'real world' from the 'ideal world', what exists from how we think it, Schelling gives an account of how they are connected. To do so, he demonstrates that the concepts that constitute the 'ideal' realm of cognition are the same as the concepts that constitute the 'real', or natural, realm of existence. Put simply, the forces that give rise to the possibility of an apple are the same forces which constitute an actual apple on a tree.

The terms he uses to make his case are as old as philosophy itself: being and non-being. Schelling's use of them in a mythical way, however, is unique and forms the basis of Tillich's use of them.[6] For Schelling, cognition is the result of two forces: infinite potential, or the inclination to resist taking form; and the finite, or limiting inclination to take form. Schelling identifies these inclinations with the terms non-being (infinite) and being (finite). The first systematic expression of this principle occurs in Schelling's philosophy of nature (*Naturphilosophie*). The primary concern of Schelling's *First Outline of a System of the Philosophy of Nature* of 1799 is to describe the relationship between humanity and nature, or mind and matter, without objectifying nature.[7] He conceptualizes nature as a dynamic, infinite process, in which 'real' manifestations, such as trees and apples, are formed by the same forces of being and non-being that form the ideas of apples and trees. In other words, the forces or impulses of being and non-being describe both 'the unconditioned' (*das Unbedingte*), the ideal ground or possibility of anything existing and everything that really exists.

For Schelling, everything that exists is only a particular form of 'the unconditioned'. This is not manifest in any one being, but is the possibility of there being anything at all, the potential of 'being-itself'. Being-itself is not a thing, but is 'activity', the interplay of the two forces of being and non-being. In later developments, Schelling describes non-being as the 'dark principle', or the abyss (*der Abgrund*), which is the resistance to taking form. Being is the light principle, the inclination to give form to infinite possibility. In the ideal realm, being and non-being are in perfect balance. However, through various mythical and natural metaphors, Schelling describes the creative manifestation of reality as a result of the interplay of being and non-being. The combination of being and non-being results in every real thing, every product of nature.[8] Because of the diversity and difference that characterizes the natural world and human cognition, being and non-being are said to be imbalanced in reality.[9] Through the inclinations of being and non-being – to become and to remain infinite – Schelling draws an ontological connection between the essential 'ground of being', or 'being-itself', and the existential realm of nature and cognition.

The question remaining, however, is why the activity of the unconditioned, of being-itself, results in the diversity of nature, and not in a completely exhaustive singularity? Schelling's early answer is focused on connecting nature and cognition. Nature is an infinite process of formation, or 'productivity', where each 'product' of nature is inclined towards, and increasingly successful at expressing, being-itself. That is, nature is a process by which the imbalanced manifestation of being and non-being in reality moves closer to the balance of being and non-being found in ideality. By virtue of being formed by the same principles of being and non-being, imperfect nature comes continually closer to achieving the balance of being and non-being found in cognition.

Eventually, the concept of productivity informs Schelling's description of the development of cognition, in the *System of Transcendental Idealism*,[10] and the implications of a self-limiting consciousness on the concept of God, explored in the *Philosophical Inquiries into the Nature of Human Freedom*.[11] The diversity and difference inherent in human nature and cognition is the result of a *freely* self-manifesting unconditioned. In his philosophy of identity (*Identitätsphilosophie*), Schelling describes the dialectical movement of the self. The initial identity of the self is singular, but in reflection upon what it is not, the self encounters disunity, difference or non-identity. However, to come to a new understanding of identity, which incorporates both a view of what the self is and what it is not, is the goal of the free consciousness, according to this stage of Schelling's philosophy.

Yet, the challenge remains to articulate the basis of human freedom which, abstractly, is the movement of the self towards disunity and, ethically, is the human capacity for evil. In so doing, Schelling also tries to retain the connection between being-itself and human being. The possibility of free action within reality must have its basis in ideality. Thus, he accounts for human freedom in terms of the self-manifesting 'absolute', a totality which makes room in itself for the free 'becoming' of its nature. The result is a description of 'the absolute', in terms of three mythical 'potencies' (*die Potenzen*) which, representing the competing inclinations of being, non-being and a return to the unity of the two, give rise to nature and cognition.

The first potency is the material cause of being; infinite potential and substance, that which is yet to be formed. Like the concept of non-being, it is the inclination 'not to be', to remain formless. As self-assertion, the first potency desires to remain potential. The second potency is the formal cause of being, autonomous will, the principle of limitation, or finitude. It has its dialectical function in the gradual subduing and rationalizing of the first. The second potency is said to give form to substance, causing the 'existence of the manifold', that which gives things and thoughts their definition.[12] For Schelling, these two potencies represent the self-asserting forces of substance and form, or the freedom of potential and the necessity of definition.

However, because of their independence, a problem emerges. The imposition of form onto what was originally formless threatens to undercut the potencies' logical independence. The dialectical struggle which results can only be mediated, according to Schelling, when the third potency emerges and introduces a balance. This final potency, which Schelling calls 'Spirit', is a result of the synthesis of the first and second potencies and is distinguished by its lack of self-assertion. It is the intentional unity of freedom and limitation. Despite the synthetic nature of the third potency, Schelling maintains that all three potencies remain logically distinct and constitute a single nature.

On one level, the potencies are meant to represent the eternally distinct yet united inclinations of God as the absolute.[13] They are a metaphor for the creative impulses of the absolute: pre-Creation potential, actual self-positing and the conscious unity of the two. Yet, the potencies must account not only for God's creating *impulses*, or 'nature', but also for God's complete freedom to create. Thus, Schelling argues that while the potencies constitute God's nature, God exercises the freedom to manifest Godself in contradiction to the 'eternal wheel' of the potencies.[14] God contains within Godself the positive – that is, distinct and self-generating – grounds of both necessity and freedom, or the inclinations to be and not to be. God's nature and God's freedom are two poles within the whole of God.[15]

The freedom of the absolute to *become* is what gives humanity its freedom, a freedom which also produces consciousness. In the created world, the third potency, Spirit, finds its fullest expression in humanity. The human creature 'reveals' the free and conscious act of God's creation, which is not logically explicable.[16] Here, too, the potencies serve as a metaphor for consciousness. The first potency corresponds to the unlimited potential of the intellect, while the second represents the limitation of autonomous will exerted over that potential. All cognition occurs by the interaction of these two potencies, according to Schelling. As with the 'productivity' principle of Schelling's earlier *Naturphilosophie*, cognition is the result of a constant delimitation of, or giving of form to, what is infinite. However, within the freedom of consciousness comes an awareness of finitude.

The 'becoming' of the potencies is the source of human awareness and estrangement. For Schelling, history becomes the process by which the will of God is reunited with the 'fallen' world.[17] Progress towards this reconciliation is synonymous with progress towards the culmination of revelation and consciousness.[18]

It is important to note that Schelling argues that being and non-being, and later God's nature and God's freedom, do not represent a dualism in God, or a dualism of gods, that is a progenitor of completeness and a progenitor of privation. Rather, the two principles require each other.[19] The principle of limitation requires the possibility of unlimited potential in order to posit itself. God contains the ground for both, but remains a monism. Throughout his writing, Schelling is concerned not only to describe the connection between the ideal and real worlds, but also to account for *why* what is infinite would accept finite form. That is, Schelling wonders why God would decide to become manifest, to reveal Godself.[20] In the end, he argues for the distinction between God's nature and God's freedom because God's decision to manifest must be free, not compelled.[21] Therefore, for Schelling, God encompasses both the ground of being, which is the interplay of being and non-being, and freedom. The reason for this division within Godself is that in order for the world to be created by God and yet exist as distinct from God it must be said to have its basis in something which is in God, but which is not God himself.[22]

Implications for understanding Tillich

This brief description of Schelling's ontological approach demonstrates three central influences that he had on Tillich. First, Schelling underscores the connection between nature and cognition, God and humanity. As a result of being created in God's image, humanity also has within it the impulses of being and non-being, and the freedom to act in ways that manifest these impulses.[23] The difference is that, while in God the light and dark impulses to be and not to be are in perfect balance, in humans they are not. Second, the disunity of being and non-being in humanity results in a wilfulness – the elevation of self above unity. Selfhood is a breaking off and falling away from the original unity of the absolute.[24] Though for Schelling real evil 'arises from one's heart' and not from the depth that is God's essence,[25] the conditions for the possibility of evil come from these depths. In God, they are eternally united, but in becoming in the human, the conditions can be torn apart and can become evil.

Third, Schelling maintains that human selfhood represents an ontological condition and not a moral decision. If all cognition, including the choice of evil, is ontologically rooted, then evil is a privation of what was once absolute, the division of what was once unity. We have seen that estrangement as an ontological condition causes problems for Tillich where the doctrine of creation is concerned. If finitude is not only a fall away from the absolute, but also a necessary fall, then duality and evil are the unavoidable conditions of human existence, not the results of wilfulness. However, the manifest division between the infinite and the finite also implies, both for Schelling and for Tillich, a prior unity. It is of primary importance for Tillich that human freedom, even when it chooses evil, maintains a relationship to the divine condition, which is the absolute condition. In this way, there remains, always, the possibility of the reconciliation of human existence with its essential nature.

Clearly, Tillich's ontology is influenced by Schelling. For both, the polarity of being and non-being is constitutive of the balanced and unconditioned ground of being, or being-itself, and also of imbalanced reality, both natural and existential. This even causes a similar problem in Schelling and Tillich: that the evil characteristic of finite human freedom is an ontological condition. For Schelling, the selfhood characteristic of existence is the natural result of being. For Tillich, the primary result of being human, and therefore fallen, is the sinful self-elevation of unbelief, hubris and concupiscence. However, Tillich fundamentally differs from Schelling in his understanding of what the ontological condition implies for history.

For Schelling, the aim of philosophy is to give an account of the connection between the ideal and the real, between nature and cognition. In his *Naturphilosophie*, Schelling argues that the real expression of the ideal is a process of productivity; nature moves towards an ever-closer manifestation of the ideal. That is, the goal of unity, between the ideal and the real, is contained within the process of nature itself. This concept of a *telos* internal to nature and existence carries into Schelling's descriptions of both consciousness and freedom. For Tillich, however, the *telos* of existence has to come from outside the polarity of being and non-being that characterizes humanity's conflicted state. This is because the 'conditions of existence', the imbalance of being and non-being that is common to

Schelling as well, are too overwhelming for fallen human thought and activity. The freedom which humanity inherits from God is finite and is not powerful enough to overcome the temptation to self-elevation that Tillich identifies with sin. Only a new revelation of being-itself, guided by an ecstatic reason, can offer direction in the human quest for meaning that transcends the limitations of existence.

For Tillich, nature and cognition do not move closer to being-itself through increasingly authentic productivity, and identity – or unity of opposites – does not occur within the dialectical polarity of existence. Rather, the power of being-itself grasps humanity again through revelation. There is at least one instance where Tillich has argued against an interpretation of his system in terms of Schelling.[26] Despite the terminological and conceptual similarities, Tillich says that the ontological polarities he uses to describe the human condition differ substantially from the potencies Schelling uses to describe the ideal foundation of being. To Tillich's mind, 'the potencies' are hierarchical; the second potency – associated with light, being and form – is preferable to the first potency – associated with darkness, non-being and formlessness. The third potency ensures a hierarchy, by being preferable to both the first and the second, as the potency of Spirit, unity and life.

Tillich's polarities of being, like 'freedom and destiny', however, are intentionally equally weighted and even mutually dependent. Polarities, for Tillich, 'remain on the same level'. Being precedes non-being in ontological validity, which is to say that non-being requires a concept of being in order to distinguish itself; but they are logically distinct and interdependent, not prioritized in a developmental account as they are in Schelling. Most importantly, Tillich's being-itself, which is the power and unity of being and non-being, is not the natural result of a struggle between being and non-being, as it is in Schelling, but is the unity of them.

Finally, like Schelling's productive ground, the polar elements of being and non-being in the divine ground of being are responsible for the constitution of human existence. Unlike Schelling's *Freiheitsphilosophie*, however, for Tillich, God's freedom to create is not distinct and posited against God's 'nature'; God and God's actualization are the same thing. This is expressed in the concept of infinity and in the identification of God as 'the power of being-itself'. The power of being-itself is not only in being the essential ground of existence, that is in being the ideal basis of real manifestation, as it is in Schelling.

Rather, for Tillich the power of being-itself is also in its capacity to compel finitude towards transcendence, that is, in the actualization of God and communication of the *telos* of all being.

HEGEL AND THE CONCEPTUAL STRUCTURE
OF ESSENTIALIZATION

The polarity of being and non-being is constitutive both of divine being-itself and human 'being'. This dialectical pair has close ties to Schelling's organic concept of the foundation of human existence in productive forces of being and non-being. However, Tillich uses the polarity of being and non-being not only to demonstrate the ontological connection between humanity and divinity, but also to establish the intractable conflict of human existence from which it cannot extricate itself. By this description, only a new manifestation of undisrupted essence can redeem existence. Once the New Being is revealed, life continues under the dimension of the Spirit with the goal of reunification of existence with essence as its goal, or *telos*. Described in this way, the redemption of life under the dimension of the Spirit, and the more general structure of human history, are understood in terms of a process of essentialization.

The goal of all human life and history, or Eternal Life, 'depends on a creative synthesis of a being's essential nature and what it has made of it in its temporal existence'.[27] With this concept of existence as redeemed by essence, of history as the history *of salvation*, something new is added to the dialectical process that cannot be described in terms of Schelling's concept of potentiality constantly becoming actualized in the productivity of nature, the identity of self-consciousness, or the free creative actuality of God. For Tillich, the redemption of human existence by the revelation of essence occurs *in principle* in the New Being, and is continued *within* history by the Spiritual Presence, but ultimately culminates *beyond* history.

As the symbol of repaired, or redeemed, existence, Eternal Life is a concept that not only retains the reality of existence, but also elevates it beyond history by negating the negative of existence: finitude, estrangement and ambiguity are 'conquered' by essence. Tillich says that the *telos*-providing process of essentialization shares the same essence as the perfectly united, *a priori* essence. The difference between the original essence and the essence of Eternal Life is that the latter has taken up into itself everything good about existence. What was once imperfect and finite returns to its origin, to its source, and is made whole again. As some have noted, this bears more resemblance to Hegel than to Schelling. Thus, it is necessary to briefly consider Hegel's account of the activity of essence and history.

Triadic development of the concept in Hegel

The *Science of Logic* provides the most systematic outline of the Hegelian dialectic.[28] For Hegel, 'dialectic' expresses opposition in two ways. First, it is a formal moment in all thinking – the implied negative of all propositions and statements. To think 'light' implies 'dark,' or to think 'living' implies 'dying'. When the subject thinks of something, there is a first moment of 'abstract understanding', in which the essential character of a thing is given initial, though unfinished shape in the subject's mind. From this initial thought, however, there follows a realization of the opposite of this abstraction, which Hegel calls the 'dialectical negation'.[29] Second, 'dialectic' is a term that refers not only to the 'moment of negation', but also to the mutual relationship of abstraction and negation itself – the relationship that constitutes the structure of all thought and reason.

Dialectical thinking is always inclined towards unity. Because of this unity, dialectical opposition implies a possibility of union between the two elements already dependent on each other, the formal expression of which Hegel calls 'speculative positivity'.[30] Dialectical thinking therefore comprises three moments: an original thought, an inherent or implied contradiction and a concept capable of expressing both.[31] The aim of good thinking is syllogistic: to find a term that can not only encompass, but also express both terms of an opposition. An example might be to say that a person who is 'living' is also in a sense 'dying', and that the two very different concepts can be accommodated by the single concept of 'life', which includes both vibrancy and decay.

In the *Science of Logic* and its summary edition, the *Encyclopedia Logic*, dialectic is formalized into three parts, or doctrines: 'Being', 'Essence' and 'Concept'. Together, these describe the ascent of thought to the position of the 'absolute idea', or thinking fulfilled.[32] Being is the concept (*Begriff*) only as it is 'in-itself', that is as it simply is, indeterminate, unreflective and unaware. It is a definition of the absolute, and of God, but it is just 'the first simple determination' or starting point for thought; it is therefore identified with the first stage of the dialectic, the stage of the abstract understanding.[33]

As such, being is a concept meant to encompass everything. But, to say that 'the Absolute is being' is 'the most abstract and the poorest' definition possible, because it is unreflective, indeterminate and immediate. Being is an empty concept, nothing at all. So in its emptiness, the concept of being and the concept of nothing share a similar, negligible significance.[34] Being and nothing collapse into each other not because they are the same in some metaphysical sense, but because in their initial positing there is no mediating consciousness for whom their difference can be taken as such.

This is the heart of Hegel's dialectic: negation, the notion of what is logically opposite, is present in all 'universals', that is, concepts or propositions. Hegel says that 'pure being is pure abstraction, and hence it is the absolutely negative, which when taken immediately, is nothing'.[35] As an initial starting point, the term or concept of being has no content. As such, the universals 'being' and 'nothing' are equally indeterminate as initial and isolated assertions, despite the difference intended in their use. The similarity and distinction that characterizes their relationship, however, implies two things. First, it implies that these two terms will acquire fuller definition in relation to each other, that is dialectically. Second, it suggests that their acquisition of definition is an unfolding process and that the terms cannot be assumed as given, for the thinking subject, from the outset.

Hegel calls the process by which these terms, and eventually all other pairs of terms and their inherently logical opposites, acquire their identity: *Aufhebung*. This term is notorious for its multiple transliterations into English, but for Hegel it is one of philosophy's most important concepts. According to the *Science of Logic*, *Aufhebung*, or 'sublation', has two meanings: to 'preserve', or 'maintain', and to 'cause to cease', or 'put an end to'. According to the *Encyclopedia Logic*, *Aufhebung* is a process of 'immanent transcending',[36] of movement beyond the empty abstraction of universals like 'being', but not by means of external reflection or relation to something else. *Aufhebung* is transcendence that occurs as a result of the nature of the concept itself, or the internal dialectic of the concept and its implied, logical negation. An indeterminate concept, for example 'being', becomes more determinate for the thinking subject in relation to its negation, 'nothing'. The realization that the initial term and its opposite require each other for their determinacy, leads to the 'negation of negation', or the realization that opposition on its own, or 'in-itself', does not increase understanding within or of the concept. Simple negation is rejected in favour of a concept that includes both initial positing and its opposite and lifts indeterminate being into determinate being, or 'being-for-itself'; a concept that seeks greater determinacy, or definition.[37]

Because the two terms are immanent within the single universal, the nature of a universal also includes the inclination towards a higher term that can unite both poles in a single concept. In the case of being and nothing, Hegel says that they are *aufgehoben* in the concept of 'becoming'. The concept of becoming embraces both the positive potential of being and the negative limitation of being. Thus, 'becoming' is a fuller concept than either being or nothing, because it includes them both within itself. This is the process by which the subject's concept of being moves from an unreflective state to a reflective, or aware, state. The concept of becoming leads to the first determinate statement of being: being-there, or being-in-itself.

Here we see the first crucial difference between dialectic in Hegel and Schelling. For Schelling, the forces of being and non-being are distinct and self-generating. The productivity of nature and cognition is the result of this relationship and tension which, despite the logical presence of a unifying third term, remains polarized. For Hegel, however, the opposition of a concept and its inherent negation is sublated as a result of the nature of the concept itself, not by its relation to another principle outside of it. For example, in Schelling's potencies the principle of light is posited against the principle of dark, which lies outside of it. For Hegel, the principle of light contains the principle of dark within itself, and moves towards an understanding of light that includes darkness. Thus, Hegel's understanding of dialectic is not the opposition of exclusive and opposed principles, but the discovery of opposition inherent within a single principle, and its subsequent increased understanding of itself. Progress does not begin with an ideal polarity of logically and constituted terms, but as a development of a single, unfinished concept.

In the doctrine of essence, the immanent dialectic of 'pure ideas' like being becomes a posited dialectic in 'relation to another'.[38] The next stage in Hegel's philosophy of identity requires that the logical distinction within the concept be posited outside of itself in genuine relationship.[39] In Tillich's terminology, self-identity becomes self-creativity, or movement outwards. However, even the mutual and social 'otherness' by which being-itself is further determined is only ideal, or cognitively posited.[40] For the progress of the concept to continue, this relationship must be experienced in reality. The identity and difference that were only posited and logically opposed in essence receive concrete expression in the concept of 'existence'. Together they form the basis, or ground, of existence.[41]

In Hegel's terminology, existence is the subjective experience of the concept, the concept 'realized as soul, in a body'. As the experience of the concept as existence increasingly matches the previously 'ideal' concept, the culmination of the concept as 'absolute' is closer at hand.[42] Then, says Hegel, 'Things and the thinking of them are in harmony in and for themselves.' Each point of the dialectical process leads to a manifest reality: from simple being to 'being-there'; from essential identity to existential identity; and from objective identity to subjective identity. 'In this way, the method is not an external form, but the soul and the Concept of the content.'[43]

In the earlier *Phenomenology of Spirit*, a similar dialectic provided the structure of the self-conscious development of the absolute through cultural and religious history, or 'Spirit'.[44] Every age of culture and religion epitomizes a stage in the development of the increasing self-awareness of the absolute. The four stages of history are collectively referred to as 'Spirit', a term which sums up the conceptual progress of thought towards a position of 'absolute knowledge', in which human purpose is fulfilled when transcendence is reunited with immanence.

The first stage of Spirit is 'abstract self-consciousness', that is, the subject's recognition of itself as the object of thought. In the second stage, self-consciousness moves outside of itself and seeks another subject whose existence can confirm its status. Without this other, as with the empty concept, self-consciousness can be posited, but not confirmed. Spirit is this process of mutual affirmation, 'the unity of the different independent self-consciousnesses which, in their opposition, enjoy perfect freedom and independence: "I" that is "We" and "We" that is "I"'.[45]

In the third stage of Spirit's development, the fact (*Tatsache*) of posited mutual recognition translates into an act (*Tathandlung*): a deed performed. In its embodied immediacy, Spirit is the ethical life of a people, and is the objective truth and goal uniting all self-conscious subjects.[46] However, ethical activity is not the final stage of Spirit. Eventually morality is objectified, made abstract, codified and elevated to universal status. Ethics becomes the province of 'culture', says Hegel, and language the means both of transcendence and of alienation.[47] For Hegel, the reunion of transcendent Spirit with the world, or human activity, occurs in religion.[48]

The reunion of transcendence and immanence, like self-consciousness itself, occurs in stages: first, in immediate form as natural religions;[49] second, in the art and mystery religions of Greece;[50] and third, through the Roman formalization of the spiritual in the state.[51] Finally, however, reunion occurs in the Christian religion, or the 'consummate' religion of the revealed God in Christ. Hegel describes God as manifest first as essence (Father),[52] second as being-for-self in existence (Son)[53] and third as the being-for-self which knows itself in the other (Spirit).[54] Self-consciousness is expressed in terms common to the *Science of Logic*, where life is identified with self-negation, and the unity of life and death becomes the basis of unity between transcendence and immanence in the God that dies.[55]

Christianity, however, is still primarily a 'pictorial religion' which 'turns necessary relations of essential moments within the Absolute into external generative relations of paternity and sonship'.[56] The true fulfilment of Spirit occurs after religion, in philosophy. '*Geist* is reason – being-itself – become self-conscious.'[57] Once Spirit is able to conceive of its own outward manifestation without the use of pictorial representations then Absolute Knowing is achieved, which is the goal of 'Systematic Science' (*Wissenschaft*).[58] Faith becomes knowledge when the concreteness of the manifest representation, that is Christ, is negated.[59] To accomplish this, philosophy must be able to step 'outside of itself', outside of time and space, and conceptually consider what religion only considers in representations. Thus Spirit, for Hegel, is immanent and teleological, but eventually leads thinking outside the boundaries of history into the realm of pure thought.

Implications for understanding Tillich

For Tillich, the historical and living process of essentialization is teleological. Through the revelation of the Christian symbols, viewed under the dimension of Spirit, life and history are capable of transcendence. The process of essentialization implies a direction, a *telos*, for history, which is symbolized by the Kingdom of God and Eternal Life. The Kingdom of God is a symbol of an 'inner-historical' *telos*, a goal implicit in each act and moment of history. Yet, it is also the symbol of a 'trans-historical' *telos*: Eternal Life, which represents the meaning of all life and history finally fulfilled and in complete unity with the divine. Tillich describes this reunion, or reconciliation, as the negation of all that is negative in life and history: finitude, estrangement and ambiguity. Ultimately, in the 'permanent transition from temporal to eternal', the negative is defeated and what is temporal becomes 'eternal memory'.[60]

The dialectical structure employed by both Tillich and Hegel assumes that the ultimate expression of reality is included in, not erased by, the ultimate. For Tillich, this is expressed as revelation 'fulfilling' reason, not destroying it, and in essentialization as the 'elevation of the positive' and the 'judgment of the negative' of existence.[61] Like Hegel's *Aufhebung*, Tillich's essentialization expresses transcendence that includes prior expressions. The two concepts are alike in at least three other ways. First, both begin with an original or essential state which includes human history and life in the process of its completion. Second, both contend that the direction, or *telos*, of the processes by which they develop is revealed within existence. Third, both present a reunion with original essence, which is altered by and truly expressive of the infinite in its inclusion of the historical and cognitive development that occurs through finitude.[62] For Tillich, 'the new' which is produced in existence through essentialization even 'adds something' to essential being, or original essence, when it is reunited with it.

If essentialization is seen in a Hegelian light, Tillich's concept of existence runs the risk of being defined merely as the 'implied negative' of essence, such that the revelation of essence overwhelms existence, rather than redeeming it.[63] If true, this would have even greater implications for the divine life, which provides the dialectical blueprint for human life, as the second person of the Trinity would become a merely implied negative moment.[64] Yet, Tillich takes existence and history too seriously for this to be the case.[65] It is the human situation with which he is most concerned, in fact, and to this situation he feels the symbols of Christian faith are directed. Existence, in Tillich's system, whether as 'life' or 'history', never runs the risk of becoming an unreal abstraction; it is always the ambiguous reality within which finite and estranged human beings are redeemed.

Ultimately, there is a crucial difference between Tillich's concept of essentialization, or salvation, and Hegel's concept of *Aufhebung*. Hegel is concerned to demonstrate the self-sufficiency of reason and self-consciousness by offering an account in which the goal of reason is present within it, though not yet fully developed, from its inception. The goal of Tillich's entire system, however, is to demonstrate the insufficiency of human reason, in order to present revelation as a necessity for the reunion of human existence with its essence. The impetus for human existence to seek reunion with its original essence comes not from a need found within human cognition or experience itself, but from a completely 'other' revelation of essence that cannot be accounted for even by the human capacity for differentiation. In as much as Tillich's theology is existential, it remains rooted in the 'existence' of the essential among us: in Jesus the Christ, the New Being and in the Spiritual Presence.

Where Hegel's concept of 'Spirit' in the *Phenomenology* is immanent and singular, and subsumes existence within essence, for Tillich the revelation of essence within existence does not diminish, but enhances, the value of existence. In the second volume of the *Systematic Theology*, Tillich makes it clear why existentialism runs contrary to Hegel's essentialist understanding of history:

> The common point in all existentialist attacks is that man's existential situation is a state of estrangement from his existential nature. Hegel is aware of this estrangement, but believes that it has been overcome and that man has been reconciled with his true being. According to all the existentialists, this belief is Hegel's basic error. Reconciliation is a matter of anticipation and expectation, but not of reality.[66]

This is how Tillich can be an existential theologian and still make a doctrine of essence fundamentally important to his system. The *Systematic Theology* attempts to demonstrate the connection between essence and existence, between authentic human nature and estranged humanity, and between the message of revelation and the situation into which it is revealed. The concept of essentialization is not a logical culmination of dialectic in the Hegelian sense, but the *ought* of the Kingdom revealed to humanity.

CLARIFYING TILLICH'S DIALECTICAL APPROACH

There is some question as to the compatibility of dialectical thinking and Trinitarian thinking as Tillich positions them.[67] The source of this problem, however, is not Tillich's dialectical understanding of the Trinity itself. Rather, there are two related problems. The first concerns which sense of dialectic is meant to align with the pattern of Trinitarian thinking: the polarity of being and non-being, or the triadic pattern of essence, existence and essentialization? The second question concerns what is implied if the divine life is made analogous to either of these patterns of human existence and history.

The dominant dialectical pattern of the *Systematic Theology* appears to be being, non-being and being-itself, a pattern credited by many as being influenced by Schelling. We saw that Schelling describes God in terms of three potencies, or principles, which, together, constitute God's nature: being, non-being and the unity of the two. These quasi-historical and -mythical forces are also identified with the persons of the Trinity. If dialectical and Trinitarian thinking are placed side by side in Schelling, non-being is associated with the person of God the Father, the infinite and pre-creative impulse to remain absolute.

The typology of being, non-being and being-itself, in Tillich's system, is different from that in Schelling's. For Tillich, being-itself, not non-being, is the pre-creative ground of being. The opposed impulses of being and non-being constitute both balanced, divine essence and imbalanced, human existence; but as being-itself, God is 'beyond' both essence and existence. Being-itself is what is revealed to humanity in God, the infinite call; Christ the New Being of reconciled estrangement and the Spiritual Presence in history which reconciles ambiguity.

It is clear, then, that although he borrows Schelling's terminology, Tillich clearly departs both from Schelling's understanding of being and non-being and from the philosopher's systematic intentions. Like Schelling, Tillich describes the human situation as dominated by disrupted impulses (being and non-being). Unlike Schelling, for Tillich this situation does not *result in*, but is *redeemed by*, revealed, original unity (being-itself). In Tillich's dialectical understanding of the Trinity, the speculative 'negative moment' of non-being is never an independently expressed moment, but is always present and in balance with being. This dialectical relationship ultimately serves as the blueprint for all human life and history as it is redeemed by the continuing revelation of this original unity.

Being and non-being describe the balance of essence, and the imbalance of existence; being-itself describes the power of God to reveal and to redeem. Yet, the process of this redemption in the life of the individual and in history is described by a different dialectical pattern: essence, existence and essentialization. Essence is the eternal balance of being and non-being, the state of pre-Fall humanity, that is, original human nature. Existence is the state of disrupted human nature, the imbalance of being and non-being, described by Tillich in terms of finitude, estrangement and ambiguity. With the revelation of the New Being, however, humanity witnesses original, undisrupted essence *under the conditions of existence*. The possibility of the reunion of existence with its original essence is made real. The process of reconciliation, under the guidance of the Spiritual Presence, is what Tillich calls 'essentialization'. This is the subject of the entire third volume of the *Systematic Theology*: the personal and historical process by which existence is reunited with essence, represented within history by the Kingdom, and outside of history in Eternal Life.

What happens to Trinitarian thinking if it is associated with the dialectic of essentialization, and not the polarity of being and non-being? By this model, God the Father is associated with essence; God the Son, the Christ, is associated with existence; and God the Spirit is associated with the historical and living process of essentialization. Strictly speaking, if God is 'beyond' essence; and existence, then essence is associated with ideal human nature, existence with actual human nature and essentialization with the goal of human nature. In this way, each person of the Trinity is associated with revealing these stages of human nature to humanity. We have already suggested that, within Tillich's dialectically understood Trinity, there is no negative moment *per se*, even though the Christ is associated with distinction, finitude and separation from God. Rather, each stage of the dialectical unfolding of human life and history is somehow repaired by the revelation of a person of the Trinity.

However, at least one commentator has argued that a negative moment within the Trinity is useful, as long as 'negation' is clearly defined.

It is possible to say that in his obedience to the Father unto death, the Son was negating himself or his historical particularity. Furthermore, it is possible to say that when the Spirit veils itself in order to manifest the Son and the Father, the Spirit is negating itself. Furthermore, it is possible to say what is negated is not one of the persons of the Trinity, but the element of finitude which is closely related to non-being in the second person of the Trinity.[68]

This raises three points: first, applying the concept of negation to a person of the Trinity is defensible, if by it one does not mean destruction, but self-sacrifice or self-giving; second, each member of the Trinity can be described as negating itself in terms of a sacrifice of historical particularity in favour of universal divine self-manifestation; which is, for example, consistent with Tillich's concept of the sacrifice of Jesus to reveal the Christ; third, it is not necessary to assume that negation of any sort need be applied to a person of the Trinity. Tillich's eschatology suggests that the process of essentialization culminates in Eternal Life, where the confusion of being and non-being in existence is resolved, where history and the divine life are brought into unity, and what is good about existence is taken up into union with God and what is negative is, itself, negated. Thus, negation in the Trinity can refer to what, in the end, is 'left-out' in Eternal Life.

Viewed in terms of the dialectical pattern of essentialization, the relationship of the divine life to human life changes significantly. The presence of God reflects not only the finitude of humanity, but also its essential nature. The revelation of the Christ reflects not only the estrangement of existence, but also the possibility of reconciliation. The Spiritual Presence reflects not only the ambiguity of life and history, but also the process, already under way, of reuniting existence with its original essence. In relation to humanity, the persons of the Trinity are defined by concepts of self-giving, self-negation and the eventual end of negation.

Seen this way, Tillich's dialectical understanding of the Trinity and of human life moves him further away from Schelling. Although it is a term that Tillich says he borrows from Schelling, the concept of essentialization seems to lean more heavily on a Hegelian notion of the concept developing within reality than on Schelling's attempts to describe pre-cognitive ideality as the ground of reality. For Schelling, the possibility of anything real had also to be accounted for within the ideal in order to maintain the connection between the two realms. For Tillich, however, once the power of being-itself reveals itself under the conditions of existence, and the goal of reunion with original essence is perceived, the result is not a return to original essence, but something new: Eternal Life.

Taken as a whole, the *Systematic Theology* demonstrates more than the significance of Christian symbols of revelation for conflicted humanity. It also shows that human existence is transformed by what those symbols reveal. The transcendent and infinite power of being-itself is immanently manifest. The paradox of the Christ points to the dialectic of the Trinity. As a result, human life is transformed into Eternal Life, and human history is transformed into salvation history. The polarity and intractability of existence is redeemed by the dialectical movement of history towards its *telos*. Thus, the dialectical relationship between essence and existence is properly placed in a framework in which their reconciliation is achieved in history, through essentialization.

CHAPTER 7

RECEPTION

It would be impossible to conclusively describe the influence of Tillich on twentieth-century theology. The majority of critical responses to Tillich's work occurred during and immediately following the publication of each of the volumes of the *Systematic Theology*. However, to this day many publications are still devoted to understanding and attempting the repair of his work, and occasionally restating his concepts for the contemporary situation. Perhaps more so than the other dominant theologian of the past century, Karl Barth, Tillich's approach inherently provides easier middle ground for theology to interact with other fields. Because of his own interest in subjects like psychoanalysis and depth psychology, the history of religion and the relationship of Christianity to other religions and quasi-religions, and the function of art in culture, Tillich continues to appear in many arenas outside of theology. There is also a small group of philosophical responses to Tillich which consider his work in relation to traditions other than the German Idealism of Schelling and Hegel.[1]

It is still the apologetic and philosophical approach to uniquely theological issues, however, that drives the majority of Tillich scholarship. There is a vast collection of praise and complimentary work devoted to Tillich. Some of the attempts to defend and give the best possible statement of his theology are contained throughout the preceding chapters. Here, however, we focus on critical, reparative responses to Tillich's 'answering' approach to theology. Before getting to these, however, we must consider the other kind of response to Tillich's enterprise: the 'traditionalist' response.

The traditionalist response includes critiques in which the idea of theological correlation with philosophy is, itself, unwarranted. Often, for very good historical or theological reasons, commentators with this view either reject the concept of correlation out of hand, or find that Tillich's success in the enterprise is limited. At one end of the spectrum, correlative theology is seen as a dangerous attempt to synthesize theology and philosophy. The perception is that correlation compromises the strong claims of faith by referring to them through philosophical concepts. As an example, T.F. Torrance suggests that Tillich's philosophical theology is guilty not only of emptying theological concepts of their intended meaning, but also of then filling them up with a philosophical and cultural content that is detached from God. Torrance charges that Tillich makes 'faith-knowledge' symbolic and 'non-conceptual', '. . . so that if we are to pursue theology we must borrow conceptualities from philosophy or science in order to rationalize faith. That is to say, ultimately Tillich worked with a romantic, non-conceptual approach to God.'[2]

Torrance does not explain what he means by a concept, 'conceptual knowledge', 'a romantic approach to philosophy', or how Tillich's approach is 'non-conceptual'. Even less certain is how Torrance can claim that Tillich is both romantic and non-conceptual. However, Torrance's critique of Tillich is incidental to the larger purpose of the chapter in which it occurs: a description of the rationalistic 'eclipse' of God.

Nonetheless, on Torrance's view Tillich's 'rationalizing' approach to faith and doctrine involves two separate steps. The first is a reduction of faith 'knowledge' to faith 'symbols'. The second is the 'borrowing' of scientific or philosophical devices to replace 'faith knowledge' that has been reduced to symbol. Even the traditional view of the method of correlation with which we have now dispensed would not charge Tillich with the philosophical 'replacement' of faith. However, the above demonstration that theology effectively subordinates philosophy in Tillich's system is enough to challenge Torrance's concern that Tillich's method contributes to the 'eclipse of God', that is the rationalization of faith.

Perhaps the most damaging critique of Tillich's theology, from a traditionalist point of view, is one that acknowledges and appreciates Tillich's use of philosophy for theology, but finds that Tillich's theological understanding is not as strong. According to some, while his existential analysis is fulsome and even capable of reviving an understanding of the doctrine of sin in an age of relativism and meaninglessness,[3] his description of the 'healing power' of divine revelation is less than convincing. From a Roman Catholic perspective, George Tavard has said that this is a result of Tillich's lack of attention to the scriptural and traditional ground of his interpretations, and to the requirements of exegesis and history.[4] This criticism places Tillich's approach within the history of Christian theology from the early Ecumenical Councils onwards and finds his method incompatible. For example, Tavard argues that Tillich's understanding of the purpose of the doctrine of the Trinity is 'to express in embracing symbols the self-manifestation of the Divine Life to man', and counters that the *actual* purpose of the Trinitarian doctrine is 'to express the process of Divine Life within itself'.[5] The difference here seems to be more about the difference between immanent and economic concepts of the Trinity than about Tillich's interpretation of the function of doctrine being incorrect. However, Tavard's criticism highlights the challenge of accepting Tillich's contemporary analysis of Christian doctrine.

The response to Tillich's theological approach which forms the bulk of critical Tillich scholarship, however, is reparative. Although the criticism can be exhaustive and thorough, these responses are characterized by an engagement with Tillich's project of correlation and an attempt to recast parts of his system in helpful ways. As one commentator notes, 'I feel that the way of drastic criticism which I have followed is the real way of appreciating the greatness of this outstanding apologist'.[6] Many of those who engage in Tillich address the conceptual mistakes or shortcuts that occur within a correlative method and system. For example, Kenneth Hamilton has argued that Tillich defines theology and philosophy in such a way that there is no difference between them. He blames this on two factors: the 'essentialist' character of Tillich's analysis of existence, and his symbolic rendering of the Christian message. Because of these tendencies he argues that Tillich moulds the situation to fit the message, and vice versa. Correlation, then, is not the genuine fruit of comparative discussion, but 'the product of one philosophical outlook [which] fits no more than one type of theological system'.[7]

The most systematic critic of the method of correlation echoes this sentiment, arguing that in Tillich's system, philosophy and theology are not afforded sufficient autonomy.[8] For John Clayton, if question and answer are both arranged by theology, then theology becomes didactic. He therefore objects to the dominance of theology in a system where philosophy will no longer remain independent. It could be argued that, since the system intentionally gives theology an apologetic role, it is no more a critique of Tillich's system to say that it is apologetic, even didactic, than it is to say that it is theological. Tillich is didactic insofar as the object of his methodology, ultimate concern, remains the transcendent reality of divine revelation by which all reality is judged.

One could also argue that to say that Tillich intends for theology to be only didactic is to disregard his arguments concerning the self-critical capacity of the message with which theology is ultimately concerned. As early as 1935, Tillich suggests that neither the form nor the content of human discourse, neither culture nor religion, can transmit or encapsulate the 'ultimate concern' of human existence.[9] Rather, there is a third dimension beyond question and answer, beyond form and content. Throughout Tillich's career he calls this dimension, the 'beyond', by different names; early in his writings he calls it 'the Unconditioned'; in the *Systematic Theology* it is called 'the power of being-itself'. Yet, always for Tillich, this depth is the basis of all life and thought, and this is what keeps the finitude of theology and the Church from elevating itself.

The Protestant principle and the doctrine of symbols suggest that Tillich is not interested in a synthesis of theology and philosophy, nor in an inculcating theology, but rather in the self-negating power of revelation and its implications for all systems of thought. No single religion or theological approach is authoritative in itself. The methodological authority of theology resides in its symbolic representation of the transcendent meaning of human experience. The methodological authority that philosophy provides lies in its unique contribution to the analysis of the human situation. Clayton is correct in saying that the relative autonomy required for theology and philosophy to be correlated is missing from Tillich's *Systematic Theology*. However, as we have seen, Tillich is not presenting theology and philosophy as two competing sets of data, but rather presents theology as a discipline which takes the human experience of revelation as authoritative. Theology and philosophy, therefore, can provide different layers of meaning for the human experience, which are related, or correlated. However, it is not necessary that their accounts compete.

If theology and philosophy are afforded sufficient autonomy, however, the problem of how they interact within the system raises another question. For some, a clear distinction between the two disciplines will only create more problems. For example, Douglass Lewis argues that questions arising out of any non-theological context cannot be answered from of a theological context. To do this, says Lewis, 'is like a physicist asking: "What is the [physical] source of the light of the world?" and the theologian answering: "Jesus Christ is the light of the world!"'[10] Lewis contends not only that there is a problem of logical incoherency, but that transferring a concept from one context to another reduces all concepts and their 'logical environments' to one level of discourse. The criticism is not unlike Tillich's comment that philosophy and theology operate on different levels of discourse. However, clearly Tillich believes that dialogue between the two disciplines is possible and necessary, while Lewis does not.

In Tillich's defence on this point, Guyton Hammond has clarified, if not the intentions for correlation, then at least the way the method functions within the *Systematic Theology*.[11] He begins with Tillich's underlying assumption that Christian theology must seek to correlate itself with the analysis of humanity provided by existentialism. Because existence is itself the problem, or the question to be asked, Tillich does not expect that the answer can be derived from it. Although existentialism can help develop the question implied in human existence, it cannot provide answers. When this is coupled with what Hammond takes to be Tillich's assumption of the universality of estrangement and its necessity within the human condition, the prospect of finding an answer to the question of existence within existence becomes impossible.

For Tillich, the previous attempts of existential philosophers to address estrangement from within the human condition has resulted from the failure to discern either the seriousness of the human problem, the religious or quasi-religious commitments of the philosopher as a participant in a tradition, or both. As an example, Tillich argues that for Marx, the human situation is not a tragic or inevitable necessity, but is a 'special historical situation' from which humanity can rescue itself by the revolution of material and political mandates.[12] As a result of his religious commitments, Tillich recasts existentialism within a theological framework such that the formulation of questions as well as answers is of interest to theology, or is 'elevated' to the level of religious discussion. Indeed, the concept of ultimate concern suggests that any person concerned with being-itself, the ground and power of human existence, would be so inclined. In response, Lewis points out that such an 'elevation' raises the possibility that Tillich allows the questions to predetermine the answers, or vice versa.[13] Presumably, whether this is seen as a problem or simply a demonstration of theological commitment depends on the reader.

Nonetheless, the lack of precision regarding the concept of correlation as presented in the *Systematic Theology* provokes the most common criticism of Tillich: that he is frequently guilty of equivocation. For example, J. Heywood Thomas argues that the relation of both theology and philosophy to the common 'question' of being creates a tautology, where, 'the truth of the statement follows from the definition of the terms', such that 'X = Y and Z = Y so that X = Z'.[14] To say that philosophy and theology are both concerned with the question of being implies a consistent definition of 'being' for both. But what 'being' indicates is different among theologians, among philosophers and between the two disciplines.[15]

Ian Thompson suggests that Tillich's linguistic imprecision is fuelled by his ideological purpose, and is therefore a result of rhetorical persuasion, not imprecision. Thompson is not uncritical; he suggests that Tillich's use of the term *unbedingte* is problematic. As a noun it indicates 'the ultimate', 'the absolute' and 'the infinite', while in the adjectival form it indicates what is 'unconditional', 'necessary' and 'imperative'.[16] The problem is that the logical, metaphysical and moral connotations of the term *unbedingte* create an ambiguity which Tillich then exploits. It is only through this ambiguity that Tillich can connect the abyss and 'depth' of meaning with the inherent ground and structure of meaning. Though the tactic follows Kant's example of 'implying the logically necessary and metaphysically founded character of the unconditional imperative', says Thompson, it does not make its use legitimate. The problem of equivocation extends to Tillich's use of terms such as 'being-itself', 'truth', 'logic' and 'God' interchangeably.

Despite Thompson's suggestion that Tillich is concerned not with a textbook 'anatomy of truth', but with the possibility of a 'living truth', the problem of equivocation occurs in other ways. Thomas cites Tillich's occasional use of dictionary definitions or semantics as evidence of his disregard for the responsibility of bearing out his system in all its terminology. For example, Tillich argues that the ontological priority of being over non-being is predicated on the logical necessity of the term 'being' in order to articulate 'non-being', that is what is 'not' being, in opposition. Considering the debt of Tillich's ontology to Schelling, for whom non-being is logically prior to being as infinite potential, Tillich does not need to rely on the semantic priority of being over non-being in order to articulate how his concept of non-being fits into his system.

A related criticism regarding conceptual vagueness is the complaint that Tillich never explains the 'cash value' of his metaphors of question and answer, or form and content, as pertains to the relationship of religion and culture.[17] This critique expresses a desire for clarity, or non-symbolic language, which, it seems, Tillich intentionally avoids in favour of an elasticity of meaning. Tillich further demands that readers must interpret the theologian's terminology in light of the whole system, which some consider to be a weakness.[18] For Tillich, it is simply the nature of *Systematic Theology* that the solution to the problem of apparently divergent philosophical and theological interpretations of truth is observable only by means of the entire system.[19] Whether this is sufficient to defend the ambiguities in Tillich's system is ultimately up to the reader.

The most consistently criticized point of vagueness in the entire system, however, is the concept of being-itself and religious symbols. We have seen that Tillich creates a great deal of confusion with contradictory statements, in the first and second volumes of the *Systematic Theology*, concerning being-itself as a non-symbolic statement. The issue of religious language and symbolism being predicated on this statement has also generated criticism. For example, according to John Fenton, in order for Tillich's religious language to be meaningful it must refer to God as *a* being because, 'Ontological analysis which shows *that* Being-itself is cannot be separated from the metaphysical judgment of *what* Being-itself is'.[20] That is, Tillich's concern that the concept of God be transcendent of both the physical world and the limitations of human thought produces a definition of God which is more of a logical stipulation than a positive statement. William Rowe summarizes the problem as: '(1) to explicate Tillich's concept of God we must first understand what "being-itself" means; (2) being-itself is ineffable.'[21]

The possibility of referring to something of which we have an experience, but about which we do not have understanding, is the risk of faith. To some extent, the reader of the *Systematic Theology* is asked simply to assent to the concept of God as being-itself being the only possible non-symbolic statement. This stipulation is not only a logical placeholder for all the other symbolic statements of Christian theology, but also is in its own way a dogmatic assertion about how God can be the source of our being and yet not be reachable

CONCLUSION

From his early career in Germany until his final lecture in the United States, Tillich was concerned with demonstrating how the symbols of the Christian faith are relevant not only to those inside the Church, but also to the universal human condition. Beginning with a search for a middle way between a perceived dichotomy of political extremism and religious reactionism, his initial interest in religious socialism was influenced by the theological attempts at mediation of the nineteenth century. However, his expectation of *kairos*, the hope that out of the destruction of the First World War the hope of the Kingdom would break into history, disappeared with the Second World War and the horrors of the century of violence. However, the fallenness of humanity made Tillich's desire to express the meaningfulness of revelation greater. The challenge was to express a theological approach that took account of both the inevitability of human frailty and the promise of the Kingdom revealed in the Christ.

Tillich also remained committed to the task of addressing the problems facing contemporary theology. In the mature and comprehensive *Systematic Theology*, he again sought a middle way, this time between the autonomy of reason, now exemplified by logical positivism and naturalism, and the heteronomous assumptions of neo-orthodoxy, which he called 'supranaturalism'. Tillich relates theological concepts to the philosophical analysis of existence. Appealing to ontology, he describes the human capacity for sin as the result of the polar elements of being and non-being. In essence, these elements are balanced and expressive of authentic human nature; in existence, they are unbalanced, and express the intractable human situation of finitude and estrangement, as well as the polarities that circumscribe all human dynamics and form, emotionalism and rationalism, and the inclinations towards individualization and participation. Appealing to existential analysis, Tillich describes life and history, even after the revelation of the Christ, as ambiguous. The continued human attempts to transcend the polarities of existence meet with failure. Human freedom is so universally finite that, even with deliberate and self-aware development of the individual and of the community, humanity is ultimately unable to transcend its boundaries.

To this situation, however, comes revelation. The power of being-itself, expressed in the symbol of God, grasps humanity in an ecstatic experience in which reason is not destroyed, but fulfilled, or reunited with its depth. Through this experience, humanity comes to recognize not only its finitude, but also the inherent connection it has with being-itself, the ground of human being. In the symbol of the Christ, essential human nature, that is humanity conceived without limitation, sin or the estrangement of existence, is revealed. Though this moment is historical, it is also paradoxical. New Being, the *kairotic* revelation of essence under the conditions of existence, expresses the grace and freedom of God. Through the negation of finitude, or conditioned form, the infinite call of the unconditioned is revealed in one historical time and place, but for all times and places, in Jesus who sacrifices himself to demonstrate he is the Christ. Thereafter, all other religious symbols derive their authority from the symbol of self-negation, whose authority is represented by the Cross and the Resurrection.

Ultimately, however, the paradox of the Christ does not provide the model for understanding human participation in the divine life. As gracious self-giving, the Christ manifests the power of being-itself, but as the paradoxical revelation of essence under the conditions of existence, the Christ is unique New Being. However, the Christ event reveals the real possibility of reconciliation of human existence with its essence. The symbol of the Spiritual Presence communicates the power of being-itself to continue to move human existence and history towards this end, its *telos*. The process of essentialization is a historical and ongoing one, symbolized in the inner-historical vision of the Kingdom of God and the trans-historical vision of Eternal Life. In these symbols, what is negative and ambiguous about human existence is transcended and what is positive is reunited with essence. Essentialization is not a return to simple or unaltered essence, but is an expression of the actual unity of essence and existence, the fulfilment of true humanity. And it is this dialectical pattern that provides the model for understanding human participation in the divine life.

To express such a theology, Tillich turned to the philosophical systems of his early training, especially the conceptual structures of Schelling and Hegel. In them he found the concept of dialectic that would guide both his ontological doctrine of being and non-being, as well as his concept of the essentialization of human life and history. In the language of German Idealism, he found the expression of traditional doctrines in more universalizing terms, and in the Existentialism of the late nineteenth and early twentieth centuries, he saw the potential to redefine the doctrine of sin in an age of advancing secularism. In examining these themes, we have been able to clarify not only how Tillich employed some of these concepts and structures, but also how he significantly adapted them to suit his theological purpose. It is clear that Schelling's polarity of being and non-being helps Tillich to define both the balance of essence and the imbalance of existence, as well as the ontological connection between being-itself and human being that makes revelation universally meaningful. It is also clear, however, that a Hegelian notion of dialectic guides Tillich's understanding of the relationship between essence and existence, and the continued, historical process of their reunification, which Tillich calls essentialization. Important concepts such as the self-negation, characteristic of final revelation and the sublimation of negativity in trans-historical Eternal Life, also suggest at least a conceptual influence of Hegel within Tillich's understanding of dialectic and Trinitarian thinking.

Tillich's approach to theology rests on certain bold assumptions. First, the task of theology is to make it clear that revelation does not merely happen *to* humanity, but is *for* humanity. Second, this suggests that theology is not concerned with proving the existence of God, or with defending its own authority, but with demonstrating the authority of revelation through an understanding of the universal human conditions of finitude, estrangement and ambiguity. Third, religious doctrine is only helpful insofar as it is capable of communicating this authority to a given age. No doctrine or Church can escape the prophetic criticism of dependent revelation if it locates the power of revelation in Jesus the Christ. This is because the symbols of the Cross and the Resurrection guarantee that revelation is final only when conditioned form becomes transparent to unconditioned truth through self-negation. Finally, this principle is communicated through the symbols of the Christian faith; but, at all times, religion must take account of the possibility that revelation can take any form, including cultural forms. Thus, all theological reflection must involve not only prophetic critique, but also self-critical reflection.

There are difficulties not only with Tillich's proposed responses to these contexts and concerns, but also significant disagreements with his statement of the questions and problems to which his answering theology is addressed. This is due, in part, to the fact that his approach to theology arises out of specific contexts and also due, in part, to the tools he chooses to employ in response to his articulation of the tasks of theology. This does not absolve Tillich of criticism. However, the concepts of the Protestant principle and of the dialectical nature of theological discourse should be enough to demonstrate that he is very aware of the potential error of any theological project. Perhaps the greatest advantage of such an understanding is that, even in error, theological discussion continues to have value. Interestingly, it is this principle that may have the most lasting value for all theology.

NOTES

INTRODUCTION

[1] Paul Tillich, *The Interpretation of History*, pp. vii–viii.
[2] See Paul Tillich, *The Construction of the History of Religion in Schelling's Positive Philosophy: Its Presuppositions and Principles*, Victor Nuovo, trans. (Lewisburg, PA: Bucknell University Press, 1981); Paul Tillich, *Mysticism and Guilt-Consciousness in Schelling's Philosophical Development* (Lewisburg, PA: Associated University Presses, 1975); and Paul Tillich, *Main Works Volume One: Philosophical Writings*, Gunther Wenz, ed. (Berlin: De Gruyter, 1988).

CHAPTER 1: THEOLOGICAL PRINCIPLES

[1] Paul Tillich, *The Protestant Era*, p. 32, n. 1.
[2] Tillich uses the term 'Spiritual Community', which refers to more than 'the Church'. For Tillich, 'the Church' is a human endeavor and is, therefore, subject to the ambiguities of life and history. The 'Spiritual Community', however, is the community formed, both inside and outside the Church, by the unambiguous presence of God in life and history. Paul Tillich, *Systematic Theology*, Vol. *III*, pp. 149–223. See 'Salvation History and the Spiritual Presence'.
[3] Paul Tillich, *On the Boundary*, p. 68.
[4] The shift from '*super*naturalism and naturalism' to '*supra*naturalism and naturalism' is never explicitly explained. In the *Systematic Theology*, 'supranaturalism' refers to a theological approach that views all reality through the singular lens of the complete transcendence of revelation, and a 'supernatural' theological structure is the result of maintaining the dualism of a completely transcendent realm and a completely immanent realm. See Paul Tillich, *Systematic Theology*, Vol. *I*, pp. 64–65.
[5] Paul Tillich, *Christianity and the Encounter of World Religions*, p. 71.
[6] Tillich, *CEWR*, p. 66; *ST I*, pp. 64–65 As we will see, correctly or incorrectly, Tillich associates this kind of theology mostly with Karl Barth.
[7] Tillich, *CEWR*, p. 73.
[8] Tillich, *CEWR*, p. 67.
[9] Tillich, *CEWR*, pp. 70–71.
[10] Tillich, *CEWR*, p. 70.

[11] Tillich, *CEWR*, p. 78.

[12] Tillich, *CEWR*, p. 79.

[13] Tillich, *ST I*, p. 81.

[14] Tillich, *ST I*, p. 83.

[15] Tillich, *ST I*, p. 85.

[16] At least one commentator sees in Tillich's assessment of the dualism of modernity the same concern that Hegel had to 'undermine' the separation of sacred and secular. See Merold Westphal, 'Hegel, Tillich and the Secular', *The Journal of Religion* 52/3 (1972), pp. 223–239.

[17] Tillich, *PE*, p. 63.

[18] Tillich, *ST I*, p. 134.

[19] John 12:44 Emphasis is Tillich's.

[20] Tillich, *ST I*, p. 134.

[21] Tillich, *ST III*, p. 243.

[22] Tillich, *ST II*, pp. 107, 145.

[23] Tillich, *OB*, p. 136; *PE*, p. 205; *ST III*, p. 244.

[24] For a comparative analysis of the responses of Karl Barth, Rudolf Bultmann, and Paul Tillich, see Douglas J. Cremer, 'Protestant Theology in Early Weimar Germany: Barth, Tillich and Bultmann', *Journal of the History of Ideas* 56/2 (April 1995), pp. 289–307.

[25] A full account of the reaction to this lecture can be found in Wilhelm Pauck and Marion Pauck, *Paul Tillich: His Life and Thought*, pp. 68–69. The lecture is printed as 'Der Sozialismus als Kirchenfrage: Leitsätze von Paul Tillich und Richard Wegener' (1919), in *Gesammelte Werke Vol. II*, pp. 13–20.

[26] In early works, the unconditioned is referred to as the 'depth-content' of culture, or *Gehalt*. See Paul Tillich, 'Idea of a Theology of Culture', in *Gesammelte Werke IX*, pp. 11–31.

[27] Mary Ann Stenger and Ronald H. Stone, *Dialogues of Paul Tillich*, p. 165. Tillich was a Privadozent of Theology at the University of Berlin from 1919 to 1924 He was a Professor of Theology at the University of Marburg from 1924 to 1925, and a Professor of Theology at the University of Dresden and the University of Leipzig, between 1925 and 1929 His final German post was at the University of Frankfurt from 1929 to 1933, from which he was dismissed when Hitler became Chancellor of Germany. Reinhold Neibuhr convinced Tillich to join the faculty of Union Theological Seminary in New York City. Tillich lived in the United States for the rest of his life. See Pauck and Pauck, *Paul Tillich: His Life and Thought*, pp. 130–138.

[28] Scharlemann suggests that, despite enduring friendships, Tillich shared very little of his friends' theoretical approaches. See Robert P. Scharlemann, 'Totality: A Philosophical and Theological Problem between Tillich and the Frankfurt School', in Erdmann Sturm, ed. *Religion and Reflection: Essays on Paul Tillich's Theology* (Münster: LIT Verlag, 2004), p. 157.

[29] Stenger and Stone, *Dialogues of Paul Tillich*, pp. 174–175.

[30] Paul Tillich, 'Kairos and Logos', in *Gesammelte Werke IV*, pp. 43–76.

[31] Terence O'Keeffe, 'Ideology and the Protestant Principle', *Journal of the American Academy of Religion* 51/2 (June 1983) p. 290.

[32] Tillich, *OB*, p. 41.

[33] Tillich, *OB*, p. 38.

[34] Mark 12: 29–30.

[35] George Lindbeck, 'An Assessment Reassessed: Paul Tillich on the Reformation', *The Journal of Religion* 63/4 Martin Luther, 1483–1983, (October 1983) p. 379.

[36] Tillich, *OB*, p. 41.

[37] Tillich, *OB*, pp. 41–42.

[38] Tillich, *PE*, pp. 204–205.

[39] Tillich, *PE*, pp. 230–231.

[40] Paul Tillich, 'Religion and Secular Culture', *The Journal of Religion* XXVI/2 (April 1946), pp. 79–86.

[41] Tillich, 'Religion and Secular Culture', p. 79.

[42] Paul Tillich, 'Beyond Religious Socialism', *Christian Century* 66/24 (June 1949), pp. 732–733.

[43] Tillich, *PE*, p. 246.

[44] Tillich, *PE*, p. 196.

[45] Tillich, *TC*, p. 3.

[46] Tillich, *TC*, p. 24.

[47] Tillich, *TC*, p. 23.

[48] Friedrich Schleiermacher, *The Christian Faith*, pp. 131–141, 492–495. The 'passive' and 'active' senses of awareness correspond, for Schleiermacher, to the redeeming act of the historical Christ, and the subsequent 'conversion', or continuous justification, of the faithful individual. This bears some resemblance to Tillich's concept of the Christ event as 'final' revelation, and all subsequent experiences of revelation in the faith community thereafter as 'dependent'. Tillich, *ST I*, pp. 126–128.

[49] Tillich, *TC*, p. 28.

[50] Tillich, *TC*, p. 42.

[51] Tillich, *TC*, pp. 42–43.

[52] Donald F. Dreisbach, 'Paul Tillich's Hermeneutic', *Journal of the American Academy of Religion* 43/1 (March 1975) p. 84.

[53] Tillich, *ST I*, p. 74.

[54] Tillich, *ST I*, p. 241.

[55] Tillich, *ST I*, p. 239.

[56] Mary Ann Stenger, 'Paul Tillich's Theory of Theological Norms and the Problems of Relativism and Subjectivism', *Journal of Religion* 62/4 (October 1982), p. 367.

[57] Tillich, *ST II*, p. 9.

[58] Robert P. Scharlemann, 'Scope of Systematics: An Analysis of Tillich's Two Systems', *Journal of Religion* 48/2 (April 1968), p. 140.

[59] Robert P. Scharlemann, 'Tillich's Method of Correaltion: Two Proposed Revisions', *The Journal of Religion* XLVI (1966), p. 93 In the same issue in which this article appears, a posthumously published response from Tillich confirms that Scharlemann's clarification is correct.

60 Dreisbach, 'Paul Tillich's Hermeneutic', p. 88.
61 John J. Thatamanil, 'Beyond Number: On the Relational Possibilities of Tillich's Symbolic and Speculative Trinitarianism', *Trinity and/or Quaternity: Tillich's Reopening of the Trinitarian Problem*, 2002 Proceedings of the IX International Paul-Tillich-Symposium (Münster: LIT Verlag, 2004) p. 261.
62 Tillich, *ST III*, p. 113.
63 Tillich, *ST II*, p. 219.
64 Page, 'The Consistent Christology of Paul Tillich', *Scottish Journal of Theology* 36/2 (1983) p. 198 (Author's emphasis).
65 See Dourley, 'Jacob Boehme and Paul Tillich', p. 431; Lewis S. Ford, 'The Three Strands of Tillich's Theory of Religious Symbols', *Journal of Religion* 45/1 (January 1966) p. 124; and Ian E. Thompson, *Being and Meaning: Paul Tillich's Theory of Meaning, Truth and Logic*, p. 98.
66 Tillich, *ST I*, p. 177.
67 See William L. Rowe, *Religious Symbols and God*, p. 119.
68 Dreisbach, 'Paul Tillich's Hermeneutic', p. 91.
69 Tillich, *Dynamics of Faith*, p. 51.
70 Daniel K. Calloway, 'An Analysis of the Doctrine of Revelation with Emphasis on the Perspectives of Karl Barth and Paul Tillich', *Brethren Life and Thought* XXXVII (Fall 1992) p. 241.
71 Mary Ann Stenger, 'Paul Tillich's Theory of Theological Norms and the Problems of Relativism and Subjectivism', pp. 370–372.
72 Tillich, *CEWR,* p. 73.
73 Tillich, *ST I*, p. 133.
74 Dreisbach, 'Being and Symbol, Symbol and Word', *Being versus Word in Paul Tillich's Theology*, 1998 Proceedings of the VII International Paul-Tillich-Symposium (Berlin: Walter deGruyter, 1999), p. 152. See Tillich, *ST II*, p. 166.
75 See also Donald F. Dreisbach, *Symbols & Salvation: Paul Tillich's Doctrine of Religious Symbols and His Interpretation of the Symbols of the Christian Tradition* (London: University Press of America, 1993); William L. Rowe, *Religious Symbols and God: A Philosophical Study of Tillich's Theology* (Chicago, IL: University of Chicago Press, 1968); and D. MacKenzie Brown, *Ultimate Concern: Tillich in Dialogue* (New York: Harper and Row, 1965) pp. 95–99.
76 Dreisbach, 'Being and Symbol, Symbol and Word', p. 152.
77 Tillich, *ST III*, pp. 32–50.
78 Tillich, *ST III*, pp. 50–86.
79 Tillich, *ST III*, pp. 86–106.
80 Tillich, *ST III*, p. 30.
81 A. James Reimer, 'Metaphysics and Communication', *Being versus Word in Paul Tillich's Theology*, 1998 Proceedings of the VII International Paul-Tillich-Symposium (Berlin: Walter deGruyter, 1999) p. 204.
82 Tillich, *ST III*, p. 255.
83 A. James Reimer, 'Metaphysics and Communication', p. 204.
84 Tillich, *ST I*, p. 123; *ST III*, p. 127.
85 Tillich, *ST II*, p. 125. See Pan-Chui Lai, *Theology of Religions*, p. 123.

CHAPTER 2: THEOLOGICAL METHOD

[1] Tillich, 'Beyond Religious Socialism', p. 126.

[2] Tillich, *ST I*, p. 62.

[3] Tillich, 'Beyond Religious Socialism', p. 127.

[4] Jerry H. Gill, 'Paul Tillich's Religious Epistemology', *Religious Studies* 3/2 (1967–1968) p. 477.

[5] John Powell Clayton, *The Concept of Correlation*, p. 5.

[6] Clayton, *The Concept of Correlation*, p. 16 .

[7] Clayton, *The Concept of Correlation*, p. 48.

[8] Tillich, *OB*, p. 67.

[9] Tillich, *OB*, p. 68.

[10] Tillich, *OB*, p. 98.

[11] Tillich, *OB*, p. 96.

[12] Tillich, *ST I*, p. 237.

[13] Tillich, *ST I*, p. 25.

[14] Tillich, *'Dialectic'*, p. 127.

[15] Tillich, *ST I*, p. 7.

[16] See John Webster ed. *The Cambridge Companion to Karl Barth*, pp. 13–14.

[17] Tillich, *PE*, p. ix.

[18] Tillich, *Biblical Religion and the Search for Ultimate Reality*, pp. 18–19.

[19] Tillich, *ST II*, p. 90.

[20] Tillich, *ST II*, p. 93.

[21] Tillich, *'Dialectic'*, p. 140.

[22] Tillich, *'Dialectic'*, p. 142.

[23] Tillich, *'Dialectic'*, p. 139.

[24] Tillich, *ST II*, p. 92.

[25] Tillich, *ST II*, p. 92.

[26] Tillich, *IH*, p. 32.

[27] Tillich, *'Dialectic'*, p. 127; *ST I*, p. 57.

[28] Tillich, *ST I*, pp. 56–57; 150–152.

[29] Uwe Carsten Scharf argues that Tillich's concept of paradox is linked to his concept of divine 'breakthrough', which underscores the freedom of God's action. Uwe Carsten Scharf, *The Paradoxical Breakthrough of Revelation: Interpreting the Divine–Human Interplay in Paul Tillich's Work 1913–1964* (Berlin: Walter de Gruyter, 1999) p. 8.

[30] Tillich, *ST I*, p. 64; *ST II*, pp. 90–93, 106, 108.

[31] Ian E. Thompson, *Being and Meaning: Paul Tillich's Theory of Meaning, Truth and Logic*, pp. 206–207.

[32] Kenneth Hamilton, *The System and the Gospel*, p. 209.

[33] Tillich, *'Dialectic'*, p. 127.

[34] See John P. Dourley, 'Jacob Boehme and Paul Tillich on Trinity and God: Similarities and Differences', *Religious Studies* 31/4 (December 1995) p. 440.

[35] Tillich, *ST I*, p. 8.

[36] Tillich, *ST I*, p. 8.

37 Tillich, *ST I*, p. 11.
38 Tillich, *ST I*, p. 11.
39 Tillich, *TC*, p. 22.
40 Tillich, *ST I*, p. 12.
41 Tillich, *ST I*, p. 13.
42 Tillich, *ST I*, pp. 64–66.
43 Tillich, *ST I*, p. 7.
44 Tillich, *ST I*, p. 3.
45 Tillich, *ST I*, p. 21.
46 Tillich, *ST I*, p. 131.
47 Tillich, *ST I*, p. 65.
48 Tillich, *ST I*, p. 210.
49 Tillich, *ST I*, p. 6.
50 For example, Lewis S. Ford, 'Tillich's Implicit Natural Theology', *Scottish Journal of Theology* 24/3 (1971) pp. 257–270; and Alexander J. McKelway, *The Systematic Theology of Paul Tillich: A Review and Analysis* (Richmond, VA: John Knox Press, 1964). McKelway ends most of his chapters with a reference to Tillich's 'natural theology'.
51 Tillich, *ST I*, p. 176.
52 Tillich, *ST I*, p. 62.
53 Tillich, *ST II*, p. 13.
54 Tillich, *ST III*, p. 127.
55 Clayton, *The Concept of Correlation*, p. 184.
56 Tillich, *ST I*, pp. 18–20.
57 Tillich, *ST I*, p. 22.
58 Tillich, *ST I*, p. 62.
59 Tillich, *ST I*, p. 8.
60 Tillich, *ST I*, p. 22.
61 Tillich, *ST I*, p. 24.
62 Tillich, *ST I*, pp. 20–21.
63 Tillich, *ST II*, pp. 13–14.
64 Tillich, *ST I*, p. 22.
65 Tillich, *ST I*, p. 21.
66 Tillich, *ST I*, p. 28.
67 Tillich, *ST I*, p. 6.
68 Tillich, *ST I*, p. 61.
69 Tillich, *ST I*, p. 63.
70 Tillich, *ST I*, p. 22.
71 Tillich, *ST I*, pp. 21–22.
72 Tillich, *ST I*, p. 9.
73 Tillich, *ST I*, pp. 19–20, 40, 86.
74 See Martin, *The Existentialist Theology of Paul Tillich*, p. 33; and Ford, 'Tillich's Implicit Natural Theology', *Scottish Journal of Theology* 24/3 (1971) pp. 257–261.
75 J. Heywood Thomas, *Paul Tillich: An Appraisal*, pp. 37–38.
76 Tillich, *ST I*, pp. 26–27.
77 Tillich, *ST I*, pp. 27–28.

[78] This is exemplified in Tillich's assertion that philosophers are either concerned with matters of preliminary importance, or are simply hidden theologians. (*ST I*, 25).

[79] Tillich, *ST I*, pp. 28, 124.

[80] Robert P. Scharlemann, 'The Scope of Systematics: An Analysis of Tillich's Two Systems', p. 140. Scharlemann derives his terms for first- and second-order thought, or 'religious cognition' and 'reflection on religious cognition', from Tillich's *System der Wissenschaften nach Gegenständen und Methoden*, reprinted in *Gesammelte Werke*, Vol. 1 (Stuttgart: Ev. Verlagswerk, 1959) pp. 111–293.

[81] Guyton B. Hammond, 'An Examination of Tillich's Method of Correlation', *Journal of Bible and Religion* 32/3 (July 1964) p. 251.

CHAPTER 3: BEING AND GOD

[1] The English translations of German nouns have, until recently, frequently been capitalized. Here, we will retain only Tillich's capitalizations and otherwise follow the current convention of rendering German nouns by English convention.

[2] The concept of God's self-disclosure and self-negation in the Christ, and the subsequent effect that has on history, however, also owe a conceptual debt to Hegel. See 'Philosophy and Tillich's Conceptual Structures'.

[3] Tillich, *IH*, pp. 32–33; *ST I*, p. 235.

[4] Scharlemann argues that the transition from Tillich's earlier ontology of 'the unconditioned' to his later ontology of 'unconditioned being', or 'being-itself', is likely the result of his encounter with the ontological analysis of Martin Heidegger's *Being and Time*. Scharlemann demonstrates this shift in Tillich's thought through an appeal to the early *Dogmatik*, an ontological system very different from the *Systematic Theology*. See Robert P. Scharlemann, 'Ontology in Tillich's Dogmatics of 1925', in *Religion and Reflection: Essays on Paul Tillich's Theology*, pp. 203–204.

[5] In at least one earlier work, Tillich relates the polarity of reason to cognition, arguing that the 'ego-self' is dialectically polar and that cognition is where subjective and objective meet. Tillich, 'Participation and Knowledge: Problems of an Ontology of Cognition', in Gunther Wenz, ed. *Main Works Volume One: Philosophical Writings* (Berlin: De Gruyter, 1988), p. 382. See also Tillich, *ST I*, p. 94.

[6] Tillich, *ST I*, pp. 93–94.

[7] Tillich, *ST I*, p. 71.

[8] Tillich, *ST I*, pp. 71–75.

[9] Tillich, *ST I*, p. 53.

[10] Tillich, *ST I*, p. 79.

[11] Tillich, *ST I*, p. 74.

[12] Tillich, *ST I*, p. 241.

[13] Tillich, *ST I*, pp. 108–118.

[14] Tillich, *ST I*, pp. 152–153.

15 Tillich, *ST I*, p. 189.
16 Tillich, *ST I*, p. 188.
17 Tillich, *ST I*, p. 188. The undifferentiated association of these ideas is misleading. In 'Philosophical Concepts and Structures', Hegel's concept of inherent negation is disambiguated from Schelling's notion of non-being.
18 Tillich, *ST I*, p. 189.
19 Tillich, *ST I*, p. 180.
20 Tillich, *ST I*, p. 170.
21 Tillich, *ST I*, p. 172.
22 Tillich, *ST I*, pp. 174–186.
23 Tillich, *ST I*, p. 178.
24 Tillich, *ST I*, p. 179.
25 Tillich, *ST I*, p. 184.
26 Tillich, *ST I*, p. 184.
27 Tillich, *ST I*, p. 187.
28 Tillich, *ST I*, p. 204.
29 Tillich, *ST I*, pp. 241–249.
30 Tillich, *ST I*, p. 168.
31 Tillich, *ST I*, pp. 191–198.
32 Tillich, *The Courage to Be*, p. 41.
33 Tillich, *CB*, p. 89.
34 Tillich, *CB*, p. 92.
35 Tillich, *CB*, pp. 93–114.
36 Tillich, *CB*, pp. 124–125.
37 Tillich, *CB*, p. 153.
38 Tillich, *CB*, pp. 153–159.
39 Tillich, *CB*, pp. 160–161.
40 Tillich, *ST I*, pp. 204–208.
41 Tillich, *ST I*, p. 207.
42 For discussions placing Tillich's ontological theology within historical perspective, see John P. Dourley, *Paul Tillich and Bonaventure: An Evaluation of Tillich's Claim to Stand in the Augustinian-Franciscan Tradition*, p. 39, and Donald J. Keefe, *Thomism and the Ontological Theology of Paul Tillich: A Comparison of Systems*, pp. 181–182; 331.
43 Tillich, *ST I*, p. 212.
44 Tillich, *ST I*, p. 191.
45 Tillich, *ST I*, p. 210.
46 Tillich, *ST I*, p. 241.
47 Tillich, *ST I*, p. 242.
48 Tillich, *ST I*, p. 242; *ST III*, pp. 11, 30.
49 Tillich, *ST I*, p. 242.
50 Tillich, *ST I*, p. 256.
51 Tillich, *ST I*, pp. 262, 266.
52 Tillich, *ST I*, p. 267.
53 Tillich, *ST I*, p. 251.
54 Adrian Thatcher, *The Ontology of Paul Tillich*, pp. 11–12. Thatcher distinguishes between ontology as 'quest' and as 'question', where Clayton makes the etymological argument, from the German, that Tillich means

to keep the two senses together; Clayton, *The Concept of Correlation*, pp. 180–181.

55 Thatcher credits Heidegger with the distinction between traditional and existentialist ontology. Thatcher, *The Ontology of Paul Tillich*, p. 24.

56 Alistair M. Macleod, *Paul Tillich: An Essay on the Role of Ontology in his Philosophical Theology*, p. 39.

57 Tillich, *ST I*, pp. 228–229.

58 Tillich, *TC*, pp. 25–26.

59 Macleod, *Paul Tillich*, pp. 48, 56. Macleod also refers to Bernard Martin's agreement on this criticism. Ford, 'Tillich's Implicit Natural Theology', *Scottish Journal of Theology* 24/3 (1971) pp. 261–270.

60 Tillich, *ST III*, p. 127.

61 Tillich, *CB*, p. 172.

62 John P. Dourley, 'Jacob Boehme and Paul Tillich on Trinity and God: Similarities and Differences', *Religious Studies* 31/4 (December 1995) p. 430.

63 Hamilton, *The System and the Gospel*, p. 217.

64 Gert Hummel and Doris Lax eds *Trinity and/or Quaternity: Tillich's Reopening of the Trinitarian Problem*, 2002 Proceedings of the IX International Paul-Tillich-Symposium (Münster: LIT Verlag, 2004). See Eiko Hanaoka-Kawamura, 'Das Problem der Trinität und der Quaternität bei Paul Tillich', pp. 313–318; John P. Dourley, 'The problem of the Three and the Four in Paul Tillich and Carl G. Jung', pp. 351–368; and Mary Ann Stenger, 'Quaternity versus Trinity in Tillich', pp. 319–331.

65 Thatcher, *The Ontology of Paul Tillich*, p. 87; See Tillich, *ST I*, pp. 212, 263; *ST III*, p. 344.

66 Thatcher, *The Ontology of Paul Tillich*, p. 86.

67 Tillich, *ST I*, p. 204.

68 Jean Richard, 'The Trinity as Object and as Structure of Religious Experience', in *Trinity and/or Quaternity: Tillich's Reopening of the Trinitarian Problem*, 2002 Proceedings of the IX International Paul-Tillich-Symposium (Münster: LIT Verlag, 2004) p. 22.

69 Tillich, *CB*, p. 172.

70 Tillich, *ST II*, p. 158.

71 Tillich, *ST I*, p. 136.

CHAPTER 4: EXISTENCE AND THE CHRIST

1 Tillich, *ST I*, pp. 164–165.

2 Tillich, *ST II*, p. 33.

3 Tillich, *ST II*, p. 30.

4 Tillich, *ST II*, p. 29.

5 Tillich, *ST II*, p. 33.

6 Tillich, *ST II*, pp. 47–51.

7 Tillich attributes this concept to Martin Luther. Tillich, *ST II*, p. 78.

8 The inclinations towards individualization and participation are further described in the third volume of the *Systematic Theology*, where Tillich

describes the 'ambiguity' that characterizes all human life, in terms of self-integration, self-creativity and self-transcendence. See Tillich, *ST III*, pp. 32–34.

9   Tillich, *ST II*, p. 56.
10 Tillich, *ST II*, p. 57.
11 Tillich, *ST II*, pp. 80–86.
12 Tillich, *ST II*, p. 80.
13 Tillich, *ST I*, p. 165.
14 Tillich, *ST II*, p. 14.
15 Thatcher, *The Ontology of Paul Tillich*, pp. 117–118.
16 Reinhold Niebuhr, 'Biblical Thought and Ontological Speculation', in Kegely, C.W. and Robert Bretall eds *The Theology of Paul Tillich*, p. 219. See also Blocher, Henri. 'Christian Thought and the Problem of Evil: Part II', *Churchman* 99/2 (1985) pp. 115–117; Hamilton, *The System and the Gospel*, p. 151; and R.A. Killen, *The Ontological Theology of Paul Tillich*, pp. 187–188; Martin, *The Existentialist Theology of Paul Tillich*, pp. 136–137; Thatcher, *The Ontology of Paul Tillich*, p. 133; and Thomas, *Paul Tillich: An Appraisal*, p. 132.
17 Joel R. Smith, 'Creation, Fall and Theodicy in Paul Tillich's Systematic Theology', in John J. Carey, ed. *Kairos and Logos: Studies in the Roots and Implications of Tillich's Theology* (Chicago, IL: Mercer University Press, 1978) pp. 141–165.
18 Guyton B. Hammond, 'An Examination of Tillich's Method of Correlation', p. 248.
19 Tillich, *ST I*, pp. 144–147; *ST III*, pp. 362–364.
20 Tillich, *ST III*, p. 406.
21 Tillich, *ST II*, p. 167.
22 James Luther Adams, *Tillich's Interpretation of History*, in Charles Kegley and Robert Bretall eds *The Theology of Paul Tillich*, p. 294.
23 Tillich, *ST III*, p. 369.
24 Peter Slater, 'Dynamic Religion, Formative Culture, and the Demonic in History', *Harvard Theological Review* 92/1 (1999) p. 104.
25 George Tavard, *Paul Tillich and the Christian Message*, p. 88.
26 Tillich, *The Interpretation of History*, p. 300.
27 Dreisbach, *Symbols & Salvation*, p. 187.
28 Tillich, *IH*, p. 243.
29 Tillich, *IH*, p. 250.
30 Tillich, *IH*, p. 259.
31 Tillich, *IH*, p. 256.
32 Tillich, *IH*, p. 259. The term 'fate', as used by Tillich, does not refer to an external force deciding the future. Like 'destiny' in the *Systematic Theology*, 'fate' is the collection of all our decisions; the result of making choices.
33 Tillich, *ST I*, p. 135.
34 Tavard, *Paul Tillich*, p. 98.
35 Tillich, *ST I*, pp. 126–137.
36 Tillich, *ST III*, p. 369.
37 Tillich, *ST II*, p. 150.

38 Tillich, *ST II*, p. 148.
39 Tillich, *ST II*, p. 148.
40 Tillich, *ST III*, p. 125.
41 This is likely due, to some extent, to Tillich's studies under Martin Kähler, who taught that an historical biography of Christ is impossible to construct. See Martin Kähler, *Der sogenannte historische Jesus und der geschichtliche biblische Christus* (München: Chr. Kaiser Verlag, 1953).
42 Tillich, *IH*, p. 265.
43 Tillich, *ST II*, pp. 107–118.
44 Ruth Page, 'The Consistent Christology of Paul Tillich', *Scottish Journal of Theology* 36/2 (1983) p. 205.
45 Tillich, *ST II*, pp. 108–109.
46 Cameron, Bruce J.R. 'The Historical Problem in Paul Tillich's Christology', *Scottish Journal of Theology* 18/3 (1965) p. 265; see also Hamilton, *The System and the Gospel*, p. 172; Tavard, *Paul Tillich and the Christian Message*, p. 129; Dreisbach, *Symbols and Salvation*, p. 187.
47 Bruce J.R. Cameron, 'The Historical Problem in Paul Tillich's Christology', *Scottish Journal of Theology* 18/3 (1965) pp. 260–261, 270.
48 Hamilton, *The System and the Gospel*, p. 163.
49 Michael Palmer, 'Correlation and Ontology: A Study in Tillich's Christology', *Downside Review* 96/323 (1978) pp. 122–123.

CHAPTER 5: THE SPIRITUAL PRESENCE AND TRINITARIAN THINKING

1 Tillich, *ST I*, p. 69; *ST II*, pp. 35, 80, 146; *ST III*, p. 11.
2 Tillich, *ST III*, pp. 23–24.
3 Tillich, *ST III*, p. 30.
4 Tillich, *ST III*, pp. 31–32.
5 Tillich, *ST III*, p. 32.
6 Tillich, *ST III*, pp. 109–110.
7 Tillich, *ST III*, pp. 385–388.
8 Tillich, *ST III*, pp. 388–390.
9 L. Gordon Tait, *The Promise Paul Tillich*, p. 88.
10 Tillich, *ST III*, pp. 390–391.
11 Hegel's concept of history is clarified in 'Philosophical Concepts and Structures'.
12 Tillich, *ST III*, pp. 350–355.
13 Tait, *The Promise of Paul Tillich*, p. 73.
14 Tillich, *ST III*, p. 128.
15 Tillich, *ST III*, pp. 149–161.
16 Tillich, *ST III*, p. 125.
17 Tillich, *ST III*, p. 111.
18 Tillich, *ST III*, pp. 111–129.
19 Tillich, *ST III*, p. 254.
20 Tillich, *ST III*, p. 139.
21 Tillich, *ST III*, pp. 147–148.

[22] Tillich, *ST III*, p. 377.
[23] Tillich, *ST III*, p. 244.
[24] Mary Ann Stenger, 'Being and Word in Tillich's Doctrine of Spiritual Presence', p. 288.
[25] Tillich, *ST III*, pp. 356–359.
[26] Tillich, *ST II*, p. 136.
[27] Tillich, *ST III*, p. 308.
[28] Tillich, *ST III*, p. 369.
[29] Tillich, *'Victory'*, p. 25.
[30] Tillich, *ST III*, pp. 326–331.
[31] Tillich, *ST III*, p. 329.
[32] Tillich, *ST III*, pp. 385–391.
[33] Tait, *The Promise of Paul Tillich*, p. 93.
[34] Tillich, *ST III*, p. 398.
[35] Tillich, *ST III*, p. 401.
[36] Tillich, *ST III*, p. 363.
[37] See David Kelsey, *The Fabric of Paul Tillich's Theology*, p. 82; Pan-Chui Lai, *Theology of Religions*, p. 115; Wolfhart Pannenberg, 'Review of Systematic Theology Vol. 3 by Paul Tillich', *Dialog* 14 (Summer 1965) pp. 229–232; and J Heywood Thomas, 'Introduction' in Paul Tillich ed. *On the Boundary*, p. xv.
[38] Pan-Chui Lai, *Theology of Religions*, pp. 149–151.
[39] Tillich, *ST III*, p. 144.
[40] Lewis S. Ford, 'The Appropriation of Dynamics and Form for Tillich's God', *Harvard Theological Review* 68/1 (January 1975) p. 47.
[41] Leonard F. Wheat, *Paul Tillich's Dialectical Humanism*, p. 79 On this point, Wheat is entirely alone in Tillich scholarship. Alexander McKelway is unreservedly critical of Wheat's analysis of Tillich as a disillusioned humanist, finding it to be the result of Wheat's own atheism, not Tillich's. Alexander J. McKelway, 'Book Review of 'Paul Tillich's Dialectical Humanism' by Leonard F. Wheat', *Theology Today* 28/2 (July 1971) pp. 267–269.
[42] Tillich, *ST III*, pp. 283–284 Some disagree with Tillich's interpretation of the doctrine of the Trinity. See George H. Tavard, 'A Review of *Systematic Theology, Vol. III*', *The Journal of Religion* 46/1, Part 2: In Memoriam. Paul Tillich 1886–1965 (January 1966), p. 225.
[43] Tillich, *ST I*, pp. 249–252; *ST III*, pp. 283–294.
[44] Exceptions include Pan Chui-Lai, *Towards a Trinitarian Theology of Religions. A Study of Paul Tillich's Thought* (Kampen, the Netherlands: Kok Pharos Publishing House, 1994); Randall B. Bush, *Recent Ideas of Divine Conflict. The Influences of Psychological and Sociological Theories of Conflict upon the Trinitarian Theology of Paul Tillich and Jürgen Moltmann* (San Francisco, CA: Edwin Mellon Press, 1991); and Hummel, Gert. and Doris Lax eds *Trinity and/or Quaternity: Tillich's Reopening of the Trinitarian Problem*, 2002 Proceedings of the IX. International Paul-Tillich-Symposium (Münster: LIT Verlag, 2004).
[45] Tillich, *ST III*, p. 288.
[46] Tillich, *ST III*, p. 289.

[47] Tillich, *ST III*, p. 291.
[48] Tillich, *ST I*, p. 250.
[49] Tillich, *ST III*, pp. 286–291.
[50] Tillich, *ST III*, p. 286.
[51] Tillich, *ST III*, p. 284.
[52] Tillich, *ST III*, p. 292.
[53] Robison B. James, 'Tillich's Trinity: A Venture in Pragmatism', in Gert Hummel and Doris Lax eds *Trinity and/or Quaternity: Tillich's Reopening of the Trinitarian Problem*, 2002 Proceedings of the IX. International Paul-Tillich-Symposium (Münster: LIT Verlag, 2004) p. 96.
[54] Dreisbach, 'Can Tillich have a Trinity?', in Gert Hummel and Doris Lax eds *Trinity and/or Quaternity: Tillich's Reopening of the Trinitarian Problem*, 2002 Proceedings of the IX. International Paul-Tillich-Symposium (Münster: LIT Verlag, 2004) p. 203.

CHAPTER 6: PHILOSOPHICAL CONCEPTS AND STRUCTURES

[1] Bernard Martin, *The Existentialist Theology of Paul Tillich*, p. 6 (author's Preface).
[2] Whether any of these charges is accurate has been the subject of continued debate since Hegel's death. For evidence of the diversity of current interpretation of Hegel, see the Suggested Reading list.
[3] Tillich, *ST I*, p. 86; *PE*, pp. 4, 12–15.
[4] For example, Bruce J.R. Cameron, 'The Hegelian Christology of Paul Tillich', *Scottish Journal of Theology* 29/1 (1976) pp. 27–48; Lewis S. Ford, 'The Appropriation of Dynamics and Form for Tillich's God', *Harvard Theological Review* 68/1 (January 1975) pp. 35–51; Martin Repp,'Zum Hintergrund von Paul Tillichs Korrelations-Methode', *Neue Zeitschrift für Systematische Theologie und Religionsphilosophie* 24/2 (1982) pp. 206–215; Merold Westphal, 'Hegel, Tillich, and the Secular', *The Journal of Religion* 52/3 (July 1972) pp. 223–239.
[5] Andrew Bowie, *Schelling and Modern European Philosophy: An Introduction*, pp. 12–14.
[6] Schelling's mythical expression of ontology not only owes a debt to Jakob Böhme, it also becomes stronger in his later work.
[7] Bowie, *Schelling and Modern European Philosophy*, p. 31. See F.W.J. Schelling, *First Outline of a System of the Philosophy of Nature*, Keith R. Peterson, trans. (New York: State University of New York Press, 2004) Bowie identifies this objectification with the search in post-Enlightenment natural sciences to find fixed laws and theories of nature by which cognitive judgments can be made.
[8] Bowie, *Aesthetics and Subjectivity: From Kant to Nietzsche*, p. 81.
[9] Schelling, *First Outline of a System of the Philosophy of Nature*, p. 14.
[10] See F.W.J. Schelling, *System of Transcendental Idealism*, Peter Heath, trans. (Charlottesville, VA: University of Virginia Press, 1993).
[11] See F.W.J. Schelling, *Philosophical Inquiries into the Nature of Human Freedom*, James Gutmann, trans. (Chicago, IL: Open Court Publishing, 1977).

12 Tillich, *Schelling's Positive Philosophy*, p. 16.
13 Tillich, *Schelling's Positive Philosophy*, p. 17.
14 Schelling, *The Ages of the World*, p. 97.
15 Schelling, *The Ages of the World* (author's Introduction), p. xxxix.
16 Bowie, *Schelling and Modern European Philosophy*, p. 106.
17 Tillich, *Schelling's Positive Philosophy*, p. 76.
18 Tillich, *Schelling's Positive Philosophy*, p. 78.
19 Schelling, *Of Human Freedom*, pp. 88–89.
20 Bowie refers to this as the 'problem of transition', in Schelling. Andrew Bowie, *Schelling and Modern European Philosophy*, p. 91. See also Robert P. Scharlemann, 'Tillich on Schelling and the principle of identity', *Journal of Religion* 56/1 (January 1976) p. 108.
21 Bowie, *Schelling and Modern European Philosophy*, p. 159.
22 Schelling, *Of Human Freedom*, p. 33.
23 Schelling is sometimes credited as being at the forefront of Existentialism. Søren Kierkegaard and Friedrich Engels were students of Schelling during the early phases of his 'Berlin period' (1841–1854).
24 Schelling, *Of Human Freedom*, p. 39.
25 Schelling, *Of Human Freedom*, p. 82.
26 Lewis S. Ford, 'The Appropriation of Dynamics and Form for Tillich's God', *Harvard Theological Review* 68/1 (1975) pp. 35–51.
27 Tillich, *ST III*, p. 401.
28 Peter C. Hodgson, 'Hegel's Approach to Religion: The Dialectic of Speculation and Phenomenology', *Journal of Religion* 65/2 (April 1984) p. 158. There are significant problems with the interpretation of Hegel. This is especially true where the dialectic of the 'Concept' (*Begriff*) in the *Science of Logic*, and its expression within self-consciousness in the *Phenomenology of Spirit*, are concerned. However, without adjudicating among the conflicting interpretations within Hegel scholarship, we can still gain a reasonable picture of Hegel's dialectical approach.
29 Hegel, *EL*, p. 125, §79.
30 Hegel, *EL*, p. 131, §82.
31 In the *SL*: 'quality', 'negation' and the 'negation of negation', that is, identity. In the *EL*: essential unity, or 'undifferentiated identity', non-identity, or difference, and 'the identity of identity and non-identity'.
32 In the *SL*, this division occurs as Volume I: Objective Logic, which is divided into Book 1: The Doctrine of Being, Book 2: The Doctrine of Essence; and Volume II: Subjective Logic, or The Doctrine of the Notion (or Concept). The *EL*, however, is divided into three sections: Being, Essence, and the Concept.
33 Hegel, *EL*, p. 135, §85.
34 Hegel, *SL*, p. 105.
35 Hegel, *EL*, p. 139, §87.
36 Hegel, *EL*, p. 128, §81 Zusätze.
37 Hegel, *SL*, p. 120.
38 Hegel, *SL*, p. 157, c.f. 389; Hegel, *EL*, p. 175, §112.
39 According to Beiser, this is the main problem facing all philosophers after Kant. Frederick Beiser, *German Idealism*, p. 14.

40 Hegel, *SL*, p. 396.
41 Hegel, *EL*, p. 188, §120, 121; c.f. Hegel, *SL*, pp. 444–469.
42 Hegel, *SL*, pp. 824–844; Hegel, *EL*, p. 286, §213.
43 Hegel, *EL*, p. 307, §243 Jean Hyppolite suggests that, 'The dialectic is the life of the object and dialectical thought is in no way an abstract categorization'. See Jean Hyppolite, *Studies on Marx and Hegel*, p. 9. However, the inseparability of historical 'content' from dialectical 'method' raises the problem of history being interpreted as progressivistic.
44 I employ the capitalized term 'Spirit' in accordance with its usage in scholarship on Hegel.
45 Hegel, *Phenomenology*, p. 110 Hegel's 'social' concept of self-consciousness is described more fully in a brief passage in the *Phenomenology of Spirit* entitled 'Independence and dependence of self-consciousness: Lordship and Bondage', within the section on the Truth of Self-Certainty. See Hegel, *Phenomenology*, pp. 111–119.
46 Hegel, *Phenomenology*, p. 212.
47 Hegel, *Phenomenology*, p. 308.
48 Hegel delivered a series of lectures on the philosophy of religion a number of times. The different versions of these lectures are compiled in a critical edition edited by Peter C. Hodgson. See G.W.F. Hegel, *Lectures on the Philosophy of Religion, Volume I: Introduction and the Concept of Religion, Volume II: Determinate Religion*, and *Volume III: The Consummate Religion*, Peter C. Hodgson trans., ed. (Berkeley, CA: University of California Press, 1995, 1995, 1998).
49 Hegel, *LPR II*, pp. 238–358.
50 Hegel, *LPR II*, pp. 455–497.
51 Hegel, *LPR II*, pp. 498–512.
52 Hegel, *LPR III*, pp. 189–198.
53 Hegel, *LPR III*, pp. 198–223.
54 Hegel, *LPR III*, pp. 223–247.
55 See Hyppolite, *Studies on Marx and Hegel*, p. 31.
56 Hegel, *Phenomenology*, p. 358.
57 Stephen Houlgate, *Freedom, Truth and History: An Introduction to Hegel's Philosophy*, p. 180.
58 Hegel, *Phenomenology*, p. 486.
59 Hegel, *LPR III*, pp. 220–223.
60 Tillich, *ST III*, p. 401.
61 Tillich, *ST III*, p. 398.
62 This similarity to Hegel raises a question about whether Tillich's Christology implies that the ultimate 'must' become actual through concrete expression, or whether it merely 'can' become actual through concrete expression. See Bruce J.R. Cameron, 'The Hegelian Christology of Paul Tillich', *Scottish Journal of Theology* 29/1 (1976) pp. 34–35.
63 Martin Repp, 'Zum Hintergrund von Paul Tillichs Korrelations-Methode', *Neue Zeitschrift für Systematische Theologie und Religionsphilosophie* 24/2 (1982) p. 210.
64 Thatcher, *The Ontology of Paul Tillich*, pp. 89–91.

[65] Jack Boozer, 'Being and History in Paul Tillich's Theology', *God and Being: The Problem of Ontology in the Philosophical Theology of Paul Tillich*, 1988 Proceedings of the II International Paul Tillich Symposium (Berlin: De Gruyter, 1989) pp. 143–144.

[66] Tillich, *ST II*, p. 25.

[67] Thatcher, *The Ontology of Paul Tillich*, pp. 89–91.

[68] Lai, *Theology of Religions*, p. 147.

CHAPTER 7: RECEPTION

[1] At least two responses are critical of the lack of empirical verification in Tillich's discussion of religious knowledge of revelation. Jerry Gill considers Tillich's epistemology in relation to the American liberal tradition, and William Rowe considers Tillich in relation to analytical philosophy through the concept of freedom. Jerry H Gill, 'Paul Tillich's Religious Epistemology', *Religious Studies* 3/2 (1967–1968) pp. 477–498; and William L. Rowe, 'Analytical Philosophy and Tillich's Views on Freedom', in Gert Hummel ed. *God and Being: The Problem of Ontology in the Philosophical Theology of Paul Tillich* (Berlin: Walter deGruyter, 1989), pp. 201–210. Thomas O'Meara considers the structural resemblance of Tillich's ontological system to that of Martin Heidegger. Thomas F. O'Meara, 'Tillich and Heidegger: A Structural Relationship', *Harvard Theological Review* 61/2 (1968) pp. 249–261 .

[2] Thomas F. Torrance, *God and Rationality*, p. 47.

[3] Lindbeck, 'An Assessment Reassessed: Paul Tillich on the Reformation', *Journal of Religion* 63/4, Martin Luther, 1483–1983 (October 1983) p. 383.

[4] George H. Tavard, 'A Review of *Systematic Theology, Vol. III*', p. 224.

[5] George H. Tavard, 'A Review of *Systematic Theology, Vol. III*', p. 225.

[6] J. Heywood Thomas, 'Some Aspects of Tillich's Systematic Theology', *Canadian Journal of Theology* 9/3 (July 1963) p. 165.

[7] Hamilton, *The System and the Gospel*, p. 135.

[8] Clayton, *The Concept of Correlation*, p. 189.

[9] Tillich, '*Dialectic*', pp. 128–130.

[10] Douglass Lewis, 'The Conceptual Structure of Tillich's Method of Correlation', *Encounter* 28/3 (1967) p. 269.

[11] Hammond, 'An Examination of Tillich's Method of Correlation', pp. 248–251.

[12] Tillich, *TC*, p. 103. Hammond notes that existentialists do not agree on the extent of estrangement, and that Tillich's concept of total estrangement represents an implicit critique of them, rather than simply a distinction of his definition of estrangement from theirs. Hammond, 'An Examination of Tillich's Method of Correlation', p. 249.

[13] Lewis, 'The Conceptual Structure of Tillich's Method of Correlation', p. 266. See Kenneth Hamilton, 'Tillich's Method of Correlation', *Canadian Journal of Theology* V (1959) p. 92; Bernard Martin, *The Existential Theology of Paul Tillich*, p. 34; and John Dillenberger, 'Man and the World', *The Christian Century* 76/18 (June 1959) p. 669.

NOTES

[14] J. Heywood Thomas, *Paul Tillich: An Appraisal*, p. 42.

[15] See also Macleod, *Paul Tillich*, pp. 123–130 on Tillich's ambiguous use of the word 'Love'; Ross, *The Non-Existence of God*, p. 29, on the semantics of the 'existence of God', p. 29; and Clayton, *The Concept of Correlation*, pp. 180–181 on the similarity of the terms 'quest' and 'question'.

[16] Ian E. Thompson, *Being and Meaning*, p. 95 .

[17] J. Heywood Thomas, 'Some Notes on the Theology of Paul Tillich', *Hibbert Journal* 57/3 (April 1959) p. 253; see also Hamilton, *The System and the Gospel*, p. 34, and Clayton, *Concept of Correlation*, p. 17.

[18] Hamilton, *The System and the Gospel*, p. 17.

[19] Tillich, *ST I*, p. 30.

[20] John Y. Fenton, 'Being-Itself and Religious Symbolism', *Journal of Religion* XLV/2 (April 1965) p. 74.

[21] William L. Rowe, *Religious Symbols and God: A Philosophical Study of Tillich's Theology*, p. 41. Rowe suggests that Plotinus' concept of the One helps to clarify what Tillich means by 'God is being-itself', but ultimately cannot offer any repair of the claim that God is not *a* being without simply dispensing with the claim.

SUGGESTIONS FOR FURTHER READING

TILLICH

Tillich, Paul. *The Eternal Now* (New York, NY: Charles Scribners' Sons, 1963)

Tillich, Paul. *Love, Power, and Justice: Ontological Analyses and Ethical Applications* (Oxford: Oxford University Press, 1954)

Tillich, Paul. *My Search for Absolutes*, Ruth Nanda Anshen, ed. (New York: Simon & Schuster, 1967)

Tillich, Paul. *The New Being* (New York, NY: Charles Scribners' Sons, 1955)

Tillich, Paul. *Perspectives on 19th and 20th Century Protestant Theology*, Carl E. Braaten, ed. (London: SCM Press, 1967)

Tillich, Paul. *The Shaking of the Foundations* (New York, NY: Charles Scribners' Sons, 1955)

HEGEL AND SCHELLING

Ameriks, Karl. *The Cambridge Companion to German Idealism* (Cambridge, MA: Cambridge University Press, 2000)

Beiser, Frederick C. ed. *The Cambridge Companion to Hegel* (Cambridge, MA: Cambridge University Press, 1993)

Bowie, Andrew. *Introduction to German Philosophy: From Kant to Habermas* (Cambridge: Polity Press, 2003)

Gadamer, Hans-Georg. *Hegel's Dialectic*, P. Christopher Smith, trans. (New Haven, CT: Yale University Press, 1982)

Hodgson, Peter C. *Hegel and Christian Theology: A Reading of the Lectures on the Philosophy of Religion* (Oxford: Oxford University Press, 2005)

Pinkard, Terry. *Hegel's Phenomenology: The Sociality of Reason* (Cambridge: Cambridge University Press, 1994)

Pippin, Robert B. *Hegel's Idealism: The Satisfactions of Self-Consciousness* (Cambridge: Cambridge University Press, 1989)

Taylor, Charles. *Hegel* (Cambridge: Cambridge University Press, 1977)

BIBLIOGRAPHY

PRIMARY SOURCES

Tillich

Tillich, Paul. *Biblical Religion and the Search for Ultimate Reality* (Chicago: Chicago University Press, 1955)

Tillich, Paul. *Christianity and the Encounter of World Religions* (Minneapolis, MN: Fortress Press, 1994)

Tillich, Paul. *The Construction of the History of Religion in Schelling's Positive Philosophy: Its Presuppositions and Principles*, Victor Nuovo, trans. (Lewisburg, PA: Bucknell University Press, 1981)

Tillich, Paul. *The Courage to Be* (London: Nisbet, 1952)

Tillich, Paul. *Dynamics of Faith* (New York: Harper Collins, 1958)

Tillich, Paul. *Gesammelte Werke,* 14 Bände (Stuttgart: Evangelisches Verlagswerk, 1959–1975)

Tillich, Paul. *The Interpretation of History* (London: C. Scribner's Sons, 1936)

Tillich, Paul. *Main Works Volume One: Philosophical Writings*, Gunther Wenz, ed. (Berlin: De Gruyter, 1988)

Tillich, Paul. *Mysticism and Guilt-Consciousness in Schelling's Philosophical Development* (Lewisburg, PA: Associated University Presses, 1975)

Tillich, Paul. ed. *On the Boundary: An Autobiographical Sketch* (London: Collins, 1967)

Tillich, Paul. *The Protestant Era* (Chicago, IL: Chicago University Press, 1957)

Tillich, Paul. *Systematic Theology*, Volumes I, II, and III (Chicago, IL: Chicago University Press, 1951, 1957, 1963)

Tillich, Paul. *Theology of Culture*, Robert C. Kimball, ed. (New York: Oxford University Press, 1959)

Tillich, Paul. "Victory in Defeat," *Interpretation* 6 (January 1952) 17–26

Tillich, Paul. "What is Wrong with the 'Dialectic' Theology?" *Journal of Religion* XV/2 (April 1935) 127–145

Hegel and Schelling

Hegel, Georg Wilhelm Friedrich. *The Encyclopaedia Logic (with the Zusatze)*, *Part I of "Encyclopaedia of the Philosophical Sciences,"* Geraets, Suchting and Harris, trans. (Indianapolis, IN: Hackett Publishing Co. Ltd, 1991)

Hegel, Georg Wilhelm Friedrich. *Lectures on the Philosophy of Religion, Volume I: Introduction and the Concept of Religion, Volume II: Determinate Religion, and Volume III: The Consummate Religion*, Peter C. Hodgson trans., ed. (Berkeley, CA: University of California Press, 1995, 1995, 1998)

Hegel, Georg Wilhelm Friedrich. *Phenomenology of Spirit*, Andrew V. Miller, trans., ed. (Oxford: Oxford University Press, 1979)

Hegel, Georg Wilhelm Friedrich. *Science of Logic*, Volumes I, II, and III (1812, 1813, 1816) Andrew V. Miller, trans., ed. (New York: Humanity Books, 1998)

Schelling, Friedrich Wilhelm Joseph. *The Ages of the World*, Jason M. Wirth, ed. (New York: State University of New York Press, 2000)

Schelling, Friedrich Wilhelm Joseph. *First Outline of a System of the Philosophy of Nature*, Keith R. Peterson, trans. (New York: State University of New York Press, 2004)

Schelling, Friedrich Wilhelm Joseph. *Philosophical Inquiries into the Nature of Human Freedom*, James Gutmann, trans., ed. (Chicago, IL: Open Court Publishing, 1977)

Schelling, Friedrich Wilhelm Joseph. *System of Transcendental Idealism*, Peter Heath, trans. (Charlottesville, VA: University of Virginia Press, 1993)

SECONDARY SOURCES

Tillich

Blocher, Henri. "Christian Thought and the Problem of Evil: Part II," *Churchman* 99/2 (1985) 101–130

Brown, D. MacKenzie. *Ultimate Concern: Tillich in Dialogue* (New York: Harper and Row, 1965)

Bush, Randall B. *Recent Ideas of Divine Conflict. The Influences of Psychological and Sociological Theories of Conflict upon the Trinitarian Theology of Paul Tillich and Jürgen Moltmann* (San Francisco, CA: Edwin Mellen Press, 1991)

Calloway, Daniel K. "An Analysis of the Doctrine of Revelation with Emphasis on the Perspectives of Karl Barth and Paul Tillich," *Brethren Life and Thought* XXXVII (Fall 1992) 237–250

Cameron, Bruce J.R. "The Hegelian Christology of Paul Tillich," *Scottish Journal of Theology* 29 (1976) 27–48

Cameron, Bruce J.R. "The Historical Problem in Paul Tillich's Christology," *Scottish Journal of Theology* 18/3 (1965) 257–272

Carey, John J. ed. *Kairos and Logos: Studies in the Roots and Implications of Tillich's Theology* (Atlanta, GA: Mercer University Press, 1978)

Clayton, John Powell. *The Concept of Correlation: Paul Tillich and the Possibility of a Mediating Theology* (Berlin: De Gruyter, 1980)

Cremer, Douglas J. "Protestant Theology in Early Weimar Germany: Barth, Tillich and Bultmann," *Journal of the History of Ideas* 56/2 (April 1995) 289–307

Dourley, John P. "Jacob Boehme and Paul Tillich on Trinity and God: Similarities and Differences," *Religious Studies* 31/4 (December 1995) 429–445

Dourley, John P. *Paul Tillich and Bonaventure: An Evaluation of Tillich's Claim to Stand in the Augustinian-Franciscan Tradition* (Leiden: E.J. Brill, 1975)

Dreisbach, Donald F. "Paul Tillich's Hermeneutic," *Journal of the American Academy of Religion* 43/1 (March 1975) 84–94

Dreisbach, Donald F. *Symbols & Salvation: Paul Tillich's Doctrine of Religious Symbols and His Interpretation of the Symbols of the Christian Tradition* (New York: University Press of America, 1993)

Fenton, John Y. "Being-Itself and Religious Symbolism," *Journal of Religion* XLV/2 (April 1965) 73–86

Ford, Lewis S. "Appropriation of Dynamics and Form for Tillich's God," *Harvard Theological Review* 68/1 (January 1975) 35–51

Ford, Lewis S. "The Three Strands of Tillich's Theory of Religious Symbols," *Journal of Religion* 46/1 (January 1966) 104–130

Ford, Lewis S. "Tillich's Implicit Natural Theology," *Scottish Journal of Theology* 24/3 (1971) 257–270

Gill, Jerry H. "Paul Tillich's Religious Epistemology," *Religious Studies* 3/2 (1967/1968) 476–498

Hamilton, Kenneth. *The System and the Gospel: A Critique of Paul Tillich* (London: SCM Press, 1967)

Hammond, Guyton B. "An Examination of Tillich's Method of Correlation," *Journal of Bible and Religion* 32/3 (July 1964) 248–251

Hammond, Guyton B. *Man in Estrangement: Paul Tillich and Erich Fromm Compared* (Nashville, TN: Vanderbilt University Press, 1965)

Hummel, Gert. ed. *God and Being: The Problem of Ontology in the Philosophical Theology of Paul Tillich*, 1988 Proceedings of the II International Paul Tillich Symposium (Berlin: De Gruyter, 1989)

Hummel, Gert and Doris Lax. eds *Being versus Word in Paul Tillich's Theology*, 1998 Proceedings of the VII International Paul Tillich Symposium (Berlin: De Gruyter, 1999)

Hummel, Gert and Doris Lax. eds *Trinity and/or Quaternity: Tillich's Reopening of the Trinitarian Problem*, 2002 Proceedings of the IX International Paul Tillich Symposium (Münster: LIT Verlag, 2004)

Kähler, Martin. *Der sogenannte historische Jesus und der geschichtliche biblische Christus* (München: Chr. Kaiser Verlag, 1953)

Keefe, Donald J. *Thomism and the Ontological Theology of Paul Tillich* (Leiden: E.J. Brill, 1971)

Kegley, Charles W. and Robert W. Bretall. *The Theology of Paul Tillich* (New York: Macmillan, 1952)

Kelsey, David. *The Fabric of Paul Tillich's Theology* (New Haven, CT: Yale University Press, 1967)

Killen, R. Allen. *The Ontological Theology of Paul Tillich* (Kampen: J.H. Kok N.V., 1956)

Lai, Pan-Chui. *Towards a Trinitarian Theology of Religions. A Study of Paul Tillich's Thought* (Kampen, the Netherlands: Kok Pharos Publishing House, 1994)

Lewis, Douglass. "The Conceptual Structure of Tillich's Method of Correlation," *Encounter* 28/3 (1967) 263–274

Lindbeck, George. "An Assessment Reassessed: Paul Tillich on the Reformation," *The Journal of Religion* 63/4 Martin Luther, 1483–1983 (October 1983) 376–393

Macleod, Alistair. *Paul Tillich. An Essay on the Role of Ontology in his Philosophical Theology* (London: George Allen & Unwin, 1973)

Martin, Bernard. *The Existentialist Theology of Paul Tillich* (New Haven, CT: College & University Press, 1963)

McKelway, Alexander J. "Book Review of 'Paul Tillich's Dialectical Humanism' by Leonard F. Wheat," *Theology Today* 28/2 (July 1971) 267–269

McKelway, Alexander J. *The Systematic Theology of Paul Tillich: A Review and Analysis* (Richmond, VA: John Knox Press, 1964)

O'Keeffe, Terence. "Ideology and the Protestant Principle," *Journal of the American Academy of Religion* 51/2 (June 1983) 283–305

Page, Ruth. "The Consistent Christology of Paul Tillich," *Scottish Journal of Theology* 36/2 (1983) 195–212

Palmer, Michael F. "Correlation and Ontology: A Study in Tillich's Christology," *Downside Review* 96/323 (1978) 120–131

Pannenberg, Wolfhart. "Review of Systematic Theology Vol. 3 by Paul Tillich," *Dialog* 14 (Summer 1965) 229–232

Pauck, Wilhelm and Marion Pauck. *Paul Tillich: His Life and Thought* (San Francisco: Harper & Row, 1976)

Repp, Martin. "Zum Hintergrund von Paul Tillichs Korrelations-Methode," *Neue Zeitschrift für Systematische Theologie und Religionsphilosophie* 24/2 (1982) 206–215

Richard, Jean. "The Trinity as Object and as Structure of Religious Experience," *Trinity and/or Quaternity: Tillich's Reopening of the Trinitarian Problem*, 2002 Proceedings of the IX International Paul Tillich Symposium (Münster: LIT Verlag, 2004) 19–30

Ross, Robert R.N. *The Non-Existence of God: Linguistic Paradox in Tillich's Thought* (San Francisco, CA: Edwin Mellen Press Ltd., 1978)

Rowe, William L. *Religious Symbols and God: A Philosophical Study of Tillich's Theology* (Chicago, IL: University of Chicago Press, 1968)

Scharf, Uwe Carsten. *The Paradoxical Breakthrough of Revelation: Interpreting the Divine–Human Interplay in Paul Tillich's Work 1913–1964* (Berlin: De Gruyter, 1999)

Scharlemann, Robert P. *Reflection and Doubt in the Thought of Paul Tillich* (New Haven, CT: Yale University Press, 1969)

Scharlemann, Robert P. *Religion and Reflection: Essays on Paul Tillich's Theology*, Erdmann Sturm, ed. (Münster: LIT Verlag, 2004)

Scharlemann, Robert P. "The Scope of Systematics: An Analysis of Tillich's Two Systems," *Journal of Religion* 48/2 (April 1968) 136–149

Scharlemann, Robert P. "Tillich on Schelling and the Principle of Identity," *Journal of Religion* 56 (January 1976) 105–112

Scharlemann, Robert P. "Totality: A Philosophical and Theological Problem between Tillich and the Frankfurt School," in Erdmann Sturm, ed. *Religion and Reflection: Essays on Paul Tillich's Theology* (Münster: LIT Verlag, 2004) 157–173

Schleiermacher, Friedrich. *The Christian Faith*, Hugh Ross Mackintosh and James Stuart Stewart, eds (London: T&T Clark, 1999)

Slater, Peter. "Dynamic Religion, Formative Culture, and the Demonic in History," *Harvard Theological Review* 92/1 (1999) 95–110

Stenger, Mary Ann. "Paul Tillich's Theory of Theological Norms and the Problems of Relativism and Subjectivism," *Journal of Religion* 62/4 (October 1982) 359–375

Stenger, Mary Ann and Ronald H. Stone. *Dialogues of Paul Tillich* (Macon, GA: Mercer University Press, 2002)

Tait, L. Gordon. *The Promise of Paul Tillich* (New York: J.B. Lippincott Co., 1971)

Tavard, George H. *Paul Tillich and the Christian Message* (London: Burns & Oates, 1962)

Tavard, George H. "Review of *Systematic Theology, Vol. III* by Paul Tillich," *The Journal of Religion* 46/1 Part 2: In Memoriam. Paul Tillich 1886–1965 (January 1966) 223–226

Thatcher, Adrian. *The Ontology of Paul Tillich* (Oxford: Oxford University Press, 1978)

Thomas, J. Heywood. *Paul Tillich: An Appraisal* (London: SCM Press, 1963)

Thomas, J. Heywood. "Some Aspects of Tillich's Systematic Theology," *Canadian Journal of Theology* 9/3 (July 1963) 157–165

Thomas, J. Heywood. "Some Notes on the Theology of Paul Tillich," *Hibbert Journal* 57/3 (April 1959) 250–262

Thompson, Ian E. *Being and Meaning: Paul Tillich's Theory of Meaning, Truth and Logic* (Edinburgh: Edinburgh University Press, 1981)

Torrance, Thomas F. *God and Rationality* (Oxford: Oxford University Press, 1971)

Webster, John. ed. *The Cambridge Companion to Karl Barth* (Cambridge: Cambridge University Press, 2000)

Westphal, Merold. "Hegel, Tillich, and the Secular," *The Journal of Religion* 52/3 (July 1972) 223–239

Wheat, Leonard F. *Paul Tillich's Dialectical Humanism* (Baltimore, MD: Johns Hopkins University Press, 1971)

Hegel and Schelling

Beiser, Frederick C. *German Idealism: The Struggle Against Subjectivism, 1781–1801* (Boston, MA: Harvard University Press, 2002)

Bowie, Andrew. *Aesthetics and Subjectivity: From Kant to Nietzsche* (Manchester: Manchester University Press, 1990)

Bowie, Andrew. *Schelling and Modern European Philosophy* (London: Routledge, 1993)

Hodgson, Peter C. "Hegel's Approach to Religion: The Dialectic of Speculation and Phenomenology," *Journal of Religion* 65/2 (April 1984) 158–172

Houlgate, Stephen. *Freedom, Truth and History: An Introduction to Hegel's Philosophy* (London: Routledge, 1991)

Hyppolite, Jean. *Studies on Marx and Hegel*, Mark O'Neill, trans. (New York: Basic Books, 1969)

INDEX

abgrund, der 106
absolute, the 30
  concept 116
  faith 67
  in Hegel 113–16
  idea 113
  knowledge 16, 117
  paradox 24, 77
  in Schelling 107–9, 120
  in Tillich 110, 129
abyss 96, 106, 129
alienation 117
ambiguity 16, 32, 55, 82, 84–6, 89,
  91, 99, 112, 118, 120–2
analogia imaginis 79–81, 103
Anselm 61
anxiety 24, 56, 58–61, 65, 67,
  70, 72
apologetic theology 9, 32, 39,
  41–2, 66, 81–2, 84, 124, 126–7
atheism 15
aufgehoben 115
aufhebung, Hegel's concept of 114,
  118
Augustine 56, 86
authority 16, 18, 29, 31, 44–6, 91,
  127
  of revelation 9, 13–14
autonomy 10, 18, 53, 126–7

Barth, Karl 16, 32–6, 39, 41
becoming 56, 66
being 2, 12, 22, 32, 51–75, 109–12,
  119–23

  depth of, 109–10
  essential 118
  existential 62, 70
  finite, see finitude
  and finitude 14
  ground of 13, 57, 97
  and Hegel 112–19
  human 69, 79, 84, 107, 118
  and Schelling 104–12
  subject/object, as structure
    of 56–7
  in "The Courage to Be" 58–61
  in theology and philosophy
    41–4, 46
  see also being-itself, New Being,
    non-being, ontology
being-itself 20–5, 32, 76–80,
  87–94, 109–12
  and God as 22–5, 51–4
  and power of 3, 19, 21, 31,
    52–64, 68, 70, 79, 87–94,
    111–12, 119–23
Bible 25, 39
  biblical 52, 71, 79
Böhme, Jacob 52, 56–7

categories 28, 30, 37, 39–41, 44, 52,
  54, 64
  of existence 70, 83, 85, 104
causality 70
Christ, the 21–2, 32, 64–82, 120–2
  biblical picture of *see analogia
    imaginis*
  doctrine of *see* Christology

Christ, the—(*Cont'd*)
  and existence 69–82
  as God revealed 14, 64–75, 89,
    117
  historical 73–80
  and history 73–82
  and kairos 24, 75–80
  and kingdom 89–91
  as logos 38, 42–6, 64, 76–7, 88,
    93, 97–8
  as New Being *see* New Being
  paradox of 35–6, 96, 99, 123
  and self-negation 24, 55, 88,
    104–5, 117
  and Spirit 87–8, 93–5
  and Trinity 97–9
  two natures of 96–7, 99
Christian
  church 10, 14–21, 26, 28–30,
    88–90, 99, 127
  doctrine 39, 126
  faith *see* faith
  message *see* kerygma
  philosophy 43, 45
  religion *see* Christianity
  socialism 15, 40, 78
  symbols 27, 54, 70, 80, 117, 122
Christianity 11, 29, 36–7, 39,
    45–6, 55, 66–7, 76, 82, 85,
    88–9, 96–7, 105, 117–18, 124
Christology 51, 75, 77–9, 90,
    93–5, 97
church
  early 99
  latent 29
  manifest 29
  see also spiritual community
cognition 20–1, 30–2, 36, 40–2, 46,
    52–6, 74, 95, 98, 105–11,
    115–16, 119
concupiscence 71, 110
consciousness 85, 90, 104
  of God 20

  in Hegel 112–18
  in Schelling 107–12
  in Schleiermacher 20
  see also self-consciousness
correlation, method of 23, 27–8,
    32, 37–8, 42, 46–7, 51, 65, 103,
    124–6, 128–9
"Courage to Be" 24, 28–61, 66–7,
    83–4
creation 32, 52, 57, 62–4, 71, 74,
    89, 96, 108, 110
Cross 24, 67, 77, 91
culture 10, 13–15, 18–21, 28, 30, 43,
    55, 65, 80, 88, 104, 116, 124,
    127, 130

depth
  as essence 109–10
  as meaning 129
  psychology 124
  of reason 12–4, 18, 21, 53–4, 127
destiny 57
  and freedom 57–8, 71–2, 111
dialectic 28, 53, 55–7, 84, 87,
    91–2, 94
  and essentialization 68, 70, 94,
    121
  and paradox 31, 34–6, 96, 98–9
  and polarity 32, 33, 53–60, 63,
    110–12, 123
  and Trinity 94–9
dialectical
  philosophy 30–1, 107–8, 111–19
  theology 12, 30–7, 41, 68, 70,
    72, 84, 87, 94, 99, 103–5,
    119–23
dimension 86, 94, 112, 117, 127
  of the Spirit 25, 75, 83–4, 88–9
dreaming innocence 70–1

ecstasy 54
ecumenical councils 98–9, 126
Enlightenment 12, 17

epistemology 44, 53
eschatology 122
    see also essentialization,
        salvation
essence
    in Hegel 112–13, 115–19
    in Tillich 16, 23, 29, 32, 55–8, 62,
        66, 68, 69–75, 79, 81, 82, 83,
        89–95, 103–5, 109, 120–3
essentialization
    in Tillich 32, 59, 62, 67–8, 70,
        74–6, 79, 83, 87, 89–94, 103,
        105, 112, 117–23
estrangement 24–5, 32, 41, 47,
        51, 67, 69–72, 74, 76, 79, 84,
        89, 99, 109–10, 112, 118–22,
        128
eternal life 76, 82, 89–95, 104–5,
        112, 117, 121–3
ethics 44, 116
evil 55, 107, 109–10
existence 9, 12–14, 22–4, 27,
        29–32, 35, 37–8, 40–7, 51–77,
        79, 81–2, 83, 86, 89–95, 103–5,
        111, 118–23, 126–8
    in Hegel 112, 116–19
    in Schelling 108, 110–11
existentialism 27, 60, 104, 107, 119,
        128

faith 20, 23–4, 27, 36–7, 40, 67,
        77–9, 81, 88, 90, 117–18, 125,
        130
    symbols of 19
Fall, the 32–3, 70–4, 110–11, 121
Fichte, Johann Gottlieb 105
finitude 1, 3, 5, 21, 23, 32, 36,
        43, 85, 90, 108, 111, 118,
        121–2
    as being 54, 56, 58, 62
    in Hegel 112
    in Schelling 107–8
Frankfurt School 16

freedom
    and destiny 57–8, 71, 72, 111
    finite 17, 58, 63
fundamentalism 27, 39–40

God 13, 15, 19–26, 32–7, 40–2,
        51–72, 75–8, 84–99, 109–12,
        120–2
    in Hegel 112–13, 117
    Kingdom of 15, 31–2, 54, 76–8,
        82, 85–6, 89, 90–4, 104, 117,
        119, 121
    knowledge of 34–5
    persons of 95–6
    proofs of 75
    reunion with 87
    in Schelling 107–10
    Spirit of *see* Spirit
    spiritual presence of 84–6
    see also being-itself, power of
        being-itself
Gospel 14, 37, 67, 81
grace 35–6, 76
    paradox of 83, 96, 98
ground of being *see* being, God

Hegel, Georg Wilhelm
        Friedrich 29, 56, 60, 74, 86,
        103–5, 112–19, 122, 124
Heidegger, Martin 29, 64
heteronomy 10–18, 53
historical
    criticism 14, 75, 80
    inner- 90–2, 117–18
    trans- 73, 90, 92–3, 94
history 9–11, 15, 17–18, 24, 32, 35, 52,
        54–5, 59, 64, 67, 69, 70, 73–83,
        85–7, 89, 91–9, 104, 117–23
    and Christ 73–82
    and Hegel 112–13, 116
    of salvation *see* salvation,
        essentialization
    and Schelling 109–10

holy 11–12, 17, 85
Holy Spirit *see* Spirit
hubris 13, 71, 89, 95, 110
humanism 27, 29

idealism, German 31, 53, 124
identity, philosophy of 107, 115
idolatry 14, 17, 35, 38
image of, God (*imago dei*) 32
immanence 67, 75, 86, 94–5, 105,
    114–17, 119, 123, 126
individualization 57, 59–60, 71, 83,
    86
infinity 52, 56, 61–4, 68, 111

Jesus *see* Christ
justification 60, 89

kairos (*kairoi*) 15–9, 24, 69, 75–9
    and Kingdom 76–8
Kairos Circle, the 16
Kant, Immanuel 27, 44, 105, 129
kerygma 28, 37, 39–41, 51
Kierkegaard, Søren 29, 103–4
Kingdom of God 15, 31–2, 54, 56,
    69, 76, 78, 80, 82, 85–6, 89–94,
    104, 117, 119, 121
knowledge 16, 41, 84, 98, 117, 125
    absolute 16, 116
    ontological 53–5, 58, 65
    of revelation 34–6, 52

life *see* eternal life, self-creation,
    self-integration,
    self-transcendence
logos 38, 42–6, 64, 76–7, 88, 93,
    97–8
love 76, 88–9, 95
Luther, Martin 16

method of correlation 27–8, 33, 37,
    46–7, 53–4, 125–6
mind 12, 23, 83, 93, 106, 113

miracle 54
mystery 54, 77, 96–7, 117
mysticism 66, 72
myth 20, 70–1, 80–1
    potencies as 106–7, 120

naturalism 10, 27, 38, 40, 44, 60
New Being 5, 23–4, 35, 45, 69,
    73–82, 87–90, 93–5, 119–20
Nietzsche, Friedrich 103
non-being 25, 32, 38–40, 55–8, 69,
    72–5, 109–12, 119–23
    and Hegel 113–19
    and Schelling 104–12

object 19, 24, 38, 42, 44–5, 52–4,
    57, 59, 66–7, 71, 96, 116
ontology 9, 19–20, 22–3, 31, 41,
    51–3, 55–7, 61–6, 69–70,
    74–5, 78–9, 81–2, 86, 109, 111,
    129–30
    in Hegel 112
    ontological questions 42
    ontological structure 53, 104
    in Schelling 105–6, 109–10
    see also being, being-itself, God,
        New Being, and non-being

pantheism 40, 61
paradox 31, 34–6, 98–9
    of faith 24, 34–6, 73, 77, 80, 83,
        89, 96, 98–9, 123
participation 17, 23, 25, 30, 33–5,
    37, 39, 41, 57, 59–60, 64, 68,
    71, 83, 86, 88, 91–3, 95, 99
philosophy 12, 28–30, 37–9,
    41–6, 52, 70, 73–4, 105–7, 110,
    114–15, 117, 124–9
Plato 53, 71, 73
polarity 53–7
    of being and non-being 23, 32,
        58, 63, 72, 75, 79, 87, 91,
        110–12, 115, 120–1, 123

and Hegel 112
and Schelling 110–11
self-world 59–60
politics 15–16, 18, 28–9, 90, 104,
128
positivism 44, 46
potencies, Schelling's doctrine
of 107–9, 111, 115, 120
profane 18, 29, 85
Protestant principle 10, 14–19, 24,
89, 95, 127
psychology 44, 64–5, 124

rationalism 17, 64
reason
depth of 21
existential 12–14, 32, 34, 36, 38,
40, 54, 56–7, 61, 73–4, 118–19
ontological 52–5
reconciliation 14, 32, 47, 57–8, 69,
73–4, 76, 82, 109–10, 118–19,
121–3
redemption 24, 32, 73, 112, 120
relativism 38, 53, 125
religion 55, 60, 66, 72, 85, 87–9, 96
consummate 105, 116–17
and culture 10–21, 28–30, 33,
35, 46
history of 10, 124
religious socialism 15, 18, 40
Resurrection 67, 77, 91
revelation 9–14, 16–17, 19–26,
27–9, 31–42, 44–6, 51–5,
58, 60, 62, 65–8, 69–70,
72–5, 77, 79, 81–2, 86–8,
92–9, 103, 109, 111, 120,
125, 127
dependent 77
final 77
and Hegel, 112, 117–19
and the New Being, 45, 73–5,
77–82, 87, 90, 112, 121–2
and ontology 55–8

and Schelling 109, 111
symbols of 19–26

salvation 25, 32–3, 35–7, 47, 72,
74–6, 83, 87, 89, 91–2, 94–5,
99
history of 25, 32–3, 35–7, 47, 59,
72, 74–6, 78, 82–5, 87, 89,
91–5, 99, 112, 118, 123
Schelling, Friedrich Wilhelm
Joseph 29, 31, 52, 56, 74,
103–13, 115, 120, 122, 124
Schleiermacher, Friedrich 20, 28
secular 10–12, 14, 18, 21
self
-consciousness 45, 58, 112–18
-creation 25, 84
-integration 25, 84–7
-negation 24, 55, 88, 104–5, 117
see also Christ
-transcendence 25, 62, 84, 86–7,
91
sin 26, 32–3, 35–6, 47, 51, 56,
69–76, 78, 89, 92, 111,
125
see also concupiscence,
estrangement, the Fall,
hubris, and unbelief
socialism, religious see religious
socialism
soul 71, 83, 116
Spirit 18, 24–5, 32, 42, 78–9,
83–93, 97–9, 120–2
and Christ 93–5
Christology 93–5
in Hegel 112, 116–19
spiritual community 18, 51, 67, 78,
87–91, 94–5
spiritual presence 18, 24, 32,
51–2, 83–9, 93–5, 96, 104, 112,
119–22
subject 25, 41, 53–7, 61, 65–6, 71,
81, 86–7, 89, 113–16

subject—(*Cont'd*)
and object, as structure
of being 56–7
see also object
substance 21, 23, 30, 57, 62, 70, 78,
107–8
supernaturalism 10, 27
supranaturalism 10–11, 38–40,
80
symbols 9–10, 14–15, 18–26, 30, 42,
45–6, 51–2, 54–5, 65, 67, 70,
73, 76–7, 80, 85–6, 88–96, 99,
112, 117–18, 122–3, 125–7,
130
see also Cross, and Resurrection
synthesis 44–5, 92, 108, 112, 127

telos 18, 56–7, 63, 67, 73, 76, 78,
82–3, 85, 89–95, 104, 110, 112,
117–18, 120
theism 61, 66–8
theological circle 37
theology
apologetic 39, 42
natural 40–1, 43, 65

see also Christian theology, and
Christianity
theonomy 10–18
time 39, 70, 76–8, 81, 91–2 *see also*
Kairos
transcendence 67, 75, 86, 94–5, 105,
114–17, 119, 123, 126
Trinity 23, 32, 64, 88, 94–9, 105,
118, 120–3, 126
in Hegel 118
and Kairos 15–19, 24, 69, 75–9,
81, 90–1, 94
and kingdom 76–8

ultimate concern 18–21, 38–9, 45,
95–7, 127–8
unconditioned, the 15–16, 19–22,
24, 29–30, 38, 52, 55, 65, 73,
106–7, 110, 127
unbedingte, das 106, 129
Ungrund 56, 66
Urgrund 57
Utopianism 15, 29, 40, 76, 90

word 16, 25, 54, 76, 88